ABOUT WRITING
YOUR ESSENTIAL WRITING MANUAL

ALSO BY SUZ deMELLO

Novels

Phoenix and Dragon: Romantic Suspense
The Wilder Bride: Contemporary Romance
Queen of Shadow: Futuristic Romance
Walk Like A Man: A Contemporary Romance
Fashion Victim: Romantic Suspense
Spy Game: Romantic Suspense
Wounded Warrior: A Contemporary Romance
Secret Father: A Sweet Romance
Lord Devere's Ward: Regency Romance
Love on Thin Ice: A Hockey Romance
Deadly Waters: Contemporary Romantic Suspense

Short stories
(outside of any boxed set)

Viking in Tartan
Lovers in Tartan
Highland Vampire
Sherlock's Scandal
The Romantical Groom: Being A Satyre
Toe Cleavage

The Highland Vampire series

Viking in Tartan (short story)
Temptation in Tartan
Desire in Tartan
Lovers in Tartan (short story)
Rakes in Tartan
Highland Vampire (short story)

Non-fiction

Perilous Play: The Real Fifty Shades (memoir)
About Writing: Your Essential Writing Manual

Anthologies

Six Steamy Shorties: Sexy Short Romances
Six Sizzling Shorties: Sexy Short Romances
A Fortune to Win: A Romance Miniseries

PUBLISHED AS SUE SWIFT

His Baby, Her Heart
The Ranger and the Rescue
In the Sheikh's Arms
Engaged to the Sheik

ABOUT WRITING
YOUR ESSENTIAL WRITING MANUAL

including
Plotting and Planning

and
Write This, Not That!

(both revised and with new material)

SUZ deMELLO

THE LEGAL STUFF

PRAISE FOR SUE'S BOOKS

...writing is swift and clean...
Kirkus Reviews

...is an author to watch.
Romance Reviews Today

Sue ... just gets better and better!
Romantic Times

... a master at her craft...
AOL Writers Club Romance Group

About *Plotting and Planning*

Sue has written a concise manual that is valuable for both beginning and seasoned writers. Going to write a book?
Read this first!
Author Kylie Brant

Suz deMello's PLOTTING AND PLANNING is a concise, informative, and entertaining look at writing a novel.
Author Silver James

About *Write This, Not That!*

Five stars...good advice and fun to read.
Jo Frye

Five stars... Kudos to the author for a well-written manual!
Book CraZ

Five stars from me...
useful for both new and experienced writers.
Author Catherine Cavendish

DEDICATION

For the many writers who have helped me
along my journey

SPOILER ALERT

This treatise contains references to the below-listed
works. If you have not read or seen them, be
warned—plot points of these are revealed herein.

Charlotte's Web
Gone with the Wind
Harry Potter and the Philosopher's Stone
Harry Potter and the Goblet of Fire
Star Wars (movie—Episode Three)
The Old Man and the Sea
Titanic (movie)

TABLE OF CONTENTS

PLOTTING AND PLANNING...13

WRITE THIS, NOT THAT!...81

ABOUT WRITING

PLOTTING AND PLANNING

There are three rules to writing a novel.
Unfortunately, no one knows
what they are.

--Somerset Maugham

For decades, I sensed a creative spark glowing feebly inside me. I tried everything I could to nurture that tiny ember and fan it into a blaze. I sang in concert choirs and rock bands. I painted and made craft projects; I remember buying Styrofoam balls, rick-rack and sequins one Christmas when I was about nine. I recall how great I felt when Mrs. Elliott, my friend Dru's mother, bought one of my primitive ornaments for a whole thirty-five cents.

Later I majored in art without, alas, a shred of talent at drawing. The leap from pen to brush didn't come easily—some say I never bridged that gap.

My preference for the pen was a sign I ignored or didn't know how to interpret. And unfortunately, creative writing units in middle school English classes didn't help. They never answered this basic question:

How does an author write a book?

Unfortunately for aspiring authors, this is not an easy question to answer. It's tantamount to asking, *Where do authors get their ideas?* which, believe me, is our least favorite question. I often tell people I get them at Sears—they're sold by the dozen in the basement between the barbecues and the bikes.

I needed years of study to learn how to write a story, but ideas are actually the easiest part of it. I find them almost anywhere. Maybe a magazine article about a place or event. Perhaps someone I meet or something a person says may trigger a train of thought that will eventually lead to a book. Maybe travel to someplace new ignites the creative spark that will inspire me.

Here's a better question: *What are the building blocks of plot and story?*

CHARACTER AND CONFLICT

How important are these? Quite simply: No characters, no conflict. No conflict, no plot. No plot, no story. No story, no book.

It's as simple and as difficult as that. Without characters with solid inner and outer conflicts, there's no story, because your story is the journey that the characters travel to solve their conflicts. This journey may be physical, with characters actually going somewhere (Dorothy in *The Wizard of Oz)*, or it may be emotional (Scout in *To Kill A Mockingbird*).

Diane Farr, a multi-published Regency and teen novelist says, "Conflict arises from character and plot arises from conflict. The most basic level is interesting people in an impossible situation."

Plot and story should flow naturally from the characters and their conflicts. Otherwise, the story and the events in it will seem forced.

It's crucial for us to define character and conflict. So how do writers create interesting, likable characters with conflicts that readers can relate to and understand?

Farr continues, "I always dream up great characters and then have to come up with the best/worst circumstances to drop them into – some approach it the other way round, thinking 'wouldn't it be neat if ...' and come up with a harrowing situation, then have to invent the perfect characters to tackle it. But either way, the basic building blocks of a story are interesting people thrown into an impossible situation."

It's important that these people and situations are drawn from life, not merely our imaginations. Otherwise, they will lack a sense of reality that's necessary for reader acceptance of the story, even in the most wild science fiction. So how do we do that?

We watch. We go to places where people congregate and listen to their conversations. Not only do we hear snippets of interesting dialog, but we learn about folks we might never meet. After a book or two, we've exhausted the quirks of ourselves, the people in our family, and our social circle—and do keep in mind that our friends and loved ones might not want to appear as characters in our books.

If we don't get out to observe and meet new people, our books will be populated by stereotypes we meet on television or in the movies, resulting in characters with all the depth of paper dolls. While it's true that fictional characters are often larger than life—otherwise we wouldn't want to know about them—they still must be rooted in reality, or the reader will not find them sympathetic or relatable.

For a writer, there's no substitute for people watching. And talking to others in depth provides lots of information that can be used to create realistic character motivation and behavior. I once owned a T-shirt that read,

Anything you say can and will be used in my novel. Yep, it's true.

So what do we consider when creating a character? Thus far I have hinted at four qualities: realism, likability, conflict, interest.

Realism and likability may clash with conflict and interest. A writer has to achieve a careful balance between these qualities. Too likable and real a character may result in a Mr. Milquetoast. Too much conflict and interest gives an exaggerated, overly quirky character who may be good for comic relief but not much else.

An essential aspect of good storytelling is creating characters with whom the reader can identify. The reader doesn't merely consume the information you're providing. Ideally, she should live inside her mind and heart the characters' journey toward true love, the Holy Grail or Kansas—whatever the goal of the quest might be. We want to experience the tension, joy, and sorrow of the adventure. Eliciting emotion is a fundamental skill, and by creating relatable characters in trying situations, we give the reader someone to root for, become invested in, care about enough to laugh and weep along with that character as she enjoys triumphs and overcomes setbacks.

So it's crucial for an author to carefully define character and conflict. How is that done?

Some people recommend lengthy checklists, often creating elaborate character profiles before typing a single word of their new manuscript. Others are more

[17]

casual, simply having a concept in their heads. I find it useful to create collages using photos culled from a variety of sources to show character, conflict and setting. I may write descriptive words here and there on the collage that refer to character or conflict, such as "she's keeping a secret" or "what's his game?"

What's important is that the writer know these characters down to their souls.

Then s/he must get the essential information to the reader in some subtle and interesting way. Merely *telling* the reader that Scarlett is a spoiled brat who's utterly unprepared to deal with the Civil War doesn't work. It's boring. Instead, author Margaret Mitchell *shows* us Scarlett behaving badly just a few pages into Chapter One.

If the concept of "show, don't tell" is still foreign, read Chapter One of *Self-Editing for Fiction Writers* by Browne and King.

Inner and outer conflict (internal or external conflict)

We call challenges that a character faces in her outer world "outer conflicts," or "external conflicts." Personal issues are "inner conflicts," or (you guessed it) "internal conflicts." Generally, all of your major characters should have both internal and external conflicts.

Keep in mind that a short story will have one or maybe two major characters who will need these. Don't overload a short work with too many characters with too many conflicts. Conversely, a longer work should have a clear protagonist—your major character, often called the hero—with complex conflicts, but should also contain "major minor" characters with inner and outer conflicts as well.

Let's look at a couple of good examples.

Scarlett O'Hara is a great character. Why? Her inner conflict, which she fails to understand completely, is her aspiration to be a respectable Southern aristocrat while the essence of her personality is anything but. *Gone with the Wind* traces her journey from spoiled Southern belle to responsible adult, though she never loses the impulsiveness that's her signature trait. It's a coming of age story set against the backdrop of the Civil War—and that's the outer conflict.

Harry Potter's journey is also a coming of age tale. He must grapple with the emotional fallout of his parents' tragic murders by Lord Voldemort, who also plots to kill Harry (outer conflict). Harry struggles with the terrifying truth that in order to survive, he must destroy Voldemort (inner conflict). Thus, Rowling combines inner and outer conflicts most cleverly, and the entire series is set in a compelling fantasy world.

The Potter series also includes "major minor" characters with interesting pasts and solid conflicts. Harry's mates at Hogwarts also must endure adolescence; the relationship between Hermione and Ron not only adds interest to the story but influences it here and there.

Many of us were told, somewhere along the way, that

there are only four basic plot conflicts: man against man, man against nature, man against himself, and man against society. Man against himself is what is often called internal or inner conflict, and as I've stated, the major characters in every well-written book will each exhibit an inner conflict.

Overlooking the inherent sexism in the phraseology, what's most interesting in more complex stories is more complex conflicts, conflicts that may combine two or more of the basic four. Also, a long book may have multiple protagonists and antagonists—that is, heroes and villains.

Popular fiction depends upon standard plots. A mystery will almost always start with a murder or other crime, and a sleuth, either amateur or professional, will catch the villain. This is the reason we call them "whodunits." These are overwhelmingly man against man plots.

Few pop fiction genres are so narrow. Thrillers, horror, fantasy, and science fiction may often rely most strongly on man against nature, but frequently a man against man conflict will be thrown in. For example, a mismatched group of scientists, politicians and soldiers battle against, say, a menace from Mars (man against nature) while they fight about the best way to deal with the threat (man against man).

Almost every disaster film depends upon this sort of plotting. George Romero's classic *Night of the Living Dead* is a great example, with the warring couples in the farmhouse desperately trying to stave off a zombie invasion.

The Hunger Games, 1984 and *Brave New World* exhibit man against society conflicts.

A man against himself plot is often a character study, and these books are often called "character driven" as opposed to "plot driven." This distinction is a false one because all good books have both strong characters and solid conflicts, both internal and external, which lead to interesting plots and engrossing stories.

A good example of man against himself plotting is the TV series *24*, in which Jack Bauer defeats terrorists (the external conflict—man against man) while keeping a tight leash on his psychopathy (internal conflict—man against himself). The central character in *Dexter* controls his impulse to kill (man against himself) by targeting other killers (man against man). And he must evade law enforcement, of which he is a part as a blood spatter expert—a man against society conflict.

Romances are more complex, often featuring what's called a "braided plot." A braided plot interweaves two protagonists and two antagonists—and they're the same people. Often the hero will be struggling against an internal conflict (man against himself) and against falling in love with the heroine, who may exhibit a trait that causes conflict (man against man). And the same will be true of the heroine, fighting with her inner demons as well as some aspect of the hero or his character that causes her grief. Each must follow an individual path to a shared destination. Falling in love completes the "braided" plot.

The couple's conflicts may be set against a backdrop of an outer conflict such as a murder investigation or some other external threat which, in a well-written book, will influence the course of the romance and vice versa.

A great example is the film *Mr. and Mrs. Smith*, about two assassins working secretly for different employers. The internal conflict of both husband and wife is their sagging relationship and mutual dishonesty. Then each is hired to kill the other—the outer conflict.

Romances also exhibit plots and conflicts that have become standard in the genre. Some are founded on legend, myth or fairy tale, such as *Cinderella* or *Beauty and the Beast*. Others have evolved: marriage of convenience, forbidden love, love triangle, amnesiac character and so on.

Another way of thinking about conflict and story is to consider what your character wants, and what (or who) stands between him and his goal. The more conflicted your characters are, the better, even though that may make resolving those conflicts a little more difficult for you. A good reference for this approach is Debra Dixon's *GMC: Goal, Motivation and Conflict* (1996).

Again, consider *Mr. and Mrs. Smith*. The characters are united in that they love each other and want a happy marriage—but they both would like to keep their jobs. Harry Potter would like to stay alive but—oops!—the most skilled and vile sorcerer in history wants him dead.

STORY CREATION

Pantsers versus plotters

After we've figured out our characters and their conflicts, what do we do?

Well, no one wants to live with conflict, not even people we've invented. So we have to figure out their journey from conflict to resolution. As I stated, that's their—your—story.

Authors have discovered a number of ways to create that story, and an artificial division has arisen among writers who consider this issue. Some claim that they do not plot at all, and call themselves "pantsers," i.e., they write by the seat of their pants. Some are more structured. They may depend upon detailed plotting spreadsheets, and may even use a computer program to assist the plotting process. They call themselves "plotters."

Eileen Dreyer, a pantser, says, "I am left-brain deficient, so plotting to me, which is a linear function, is like vinegar on the tongue. I know the basic picture of my book when I begin, kind of like the picture on a jigsaw puzzle box. But the only way to tell it in order is to write it. If I plot too much, first it makes me want to smash my computer into gravel, and second, I lose the reason to write. I've already told myself the story. Detailed plots disperse the fairy dust of storytelling for me."

Cassie Ryan, another pantser, writes, "I'm a brainstormer/ pantser which allows me more freedom to go with the twists and turns of my story as they happen. And the brainstorming added in allows me to think about pieces of my story still to come that I want to include - so I still have a sense of 'going somewhere' with my plot rather than just tossing words onto the page, but still free to do just that."

Others find plotting before writing essential.

Phyllis Humphrey told me, "I'm a plotter... I think mysteries require plotting. I chart the activities of my characters so the possible suspects - even though they might have motives - are actually somewhere else at the time of the crime. An author needs to know what, where and why about all suspects. Which leads to the most important question - why. The author needs to know why the killer wanted the victim dead, and why the non-guilty suspects did what they did, or went where they went. Avid mystery readers will catch an author who doesn't plot out these elements and make mistakes."

In response, romantic suspense author Kylie Brant wrote: "Well, after 31 books I haven't been caught out yet :) The fact is, I tried for years to force myself to outline, to become a plotter. But you can't change the way your mind works. Sometimes I have to go back and feed in the foreshadowing but really not that often. It's like my head knows where it's going...it just doesn't always clue me in until p.250 :)"

From Rebecca York: "I am a plotter. It would be impossible for me to write four to five books a year without plotting them out first. For plotting tips, I recommend that you think of your plot and characters at the same time. Decide which people will work best in the plot you're creating... I think that if you haven't figured out the ending of the book before you start, you can't write scenes that will smoothly move the story toward your intended conclusion. In other words, you will write scenes that you will later have to discard."

In researching this essay I learned some people call themselves "puzzlers." Silver James wrote: "I start with the frame of the story: characters, setting, and basic plot line. Then I write scenes that are important and move them around until I get them in the right order."

While poking around best-selling author Jennifer Crusie's site, I found this in the FAQs:

Do you write in chronological order?

No, I tend to think in patterns, so I need to write different pieces of the book and see what happens when I put them together. That helps me build up character arcs, although it can make plotting really difficult.

So Crusie would also be a puzzler.

Nevertheless, in my not-very-humble opinion, everyone's a plotter. Why, you ask? And if you are a so-called pantser, your tone of voice is maybe a little miffed—I notice that pantsers are very proud of their off-the-cuff approach.

However, story is something that is embedded within us. It's hardwired into our consciousness and our bodies.

Here's the deal:

All stories are one and the same. There is only one story— that is, only one story we want to read.

Joseph Campbell, the preeminent mythologist of our time, called this story "the hero's journey" in his seminal *Hero With a Thousand Faces*. He identified the components in the hero's journey, and each, or most of these, must be present in any good story. By "good story" I mean one that will grab the reader and never let go.

Excluded from this premise are experimental works and some forms of literature. But if you want to write popular fiction, a story that will resonate with readers, learn the components of the hero's journey. They are most easily absorbed via a book by Chris Vogler called *The Writer's Journey*. The first chapter is essential reading for anyone who wants to write fiction.

Hero's Journey, Writer's Journey

The journey is best understood by reference to a well-known literary or cinematic work. Vogler identified twelve essential stages (see below) and used *The Wizard of Oz, An Officer and a Gentleman,* and *Star Wars* to illustrate them. I'll use *Star Wars* as well as Rowling's *Harry Potter and the Philosopher's Stone,* along with a simple story I'm making up as I write—this is Suzie being a pantser.

The Ordinary World: Luke on Tattoine. Harry in his aunt and uncle's home, awakening in the closet under the stairs.

Or you, when you get up in the morning and prepare to start your day.

The Call to Adventure: We often call this the "inciting incident," the event or person that really jumpstarts the story. Luke finds a mysterious message hidden in R2D2, a plea from Princess Leia. Owls arrive in Surrey delivering a special letter for Harry.

You stumble into the kitchen to discover a dead body on the floor. It's your roommate.

Refusal of the Call: We are often prisoners of inertia, and so are our characters. Luke tells Obi-Wan that he can't do anything to help Princess Leia. The Dursleys, with Harry, leave Surrey to evade the flocks of letter-bearing owls.

You decide you are still hallucinating from last night's mescaline and go back to bed.

Meeting with the Mentor: Luke meets Obi-Wan. Hagrid finds Harry.

Your mother stops by and sees the corpse. She calls 9-1-1.

Crossing the Threshold: This is the place in the story when

[27]

the protagonist leaves his ordinary world and enters what Campbell called "a region of supernatural wonder."

In every book, we create a world apart from our own, even if we're writing a story set in the present day in our hometown. The world of a book, any book, isn't like our world. Our world may be cluttered with irrelevant events and people who don't impact our lives. The world a writer creates includes only those objects, events, and people who have a part in the story in some way. Everything in a story should contribute to it, from the biggest monster to the tiniest comma.

In *Star Wars*, Luke crosses the threshold when he, the robots, and Obi-wan arrive in Mos Eiseley looking for a captain to take them off-planet. After enjoying Diagon Alley, Harry travels to Hogwarts.

The police arrive and you are now embroiled in a frightening new world in which you are a murder suspect.

Tests, Allies and Enemies: Your book will be populated with minor characters and events that move the plot along. Luke encounters Imperial Stormtroopers, but also finds allies in Han Solo and Chewbacca. At Hogwarts, Harry is presented with a number of allies and tests. One early test is the decision he makes while wearing the Sorting Hat—he picks courage over ambition. He chooses his Gryffindor mates as his allies and discovers that Slytherin students are potential enemies.

You are interviewed by the police. One crusty detective seems to be on your side, but his more cynical partner thinks you're a killer. Your mom hires an attorney.

Approach to the Innermost Cave: As the story progresses, dramatic tension increases through tests until the hero is confronted by true danger. Luke is on the Death Star, trying to find Leia. Harry and his mates discover a massive, three-headed dog guarding a trapdoor.

You are booked into jail.

The Ordeal: The ordeal is often the story's midpoint, preventing what many authors call a "saggy middle." Luke and his companions face death in the trash compactor. Harry is almost killed in the Forbidden Forest by Voldemort's shade.

You're attacked in a holding cell by your roommate's murderer. You defeat him.

The Reward: Our protagonists have good reason to face tests and ordeals, and the reward may be that reason. Luke rescues Princess Leia. Harry learns that the Philosopher's Stone is hidden in Hogwarts Castle and is sought by Voldemort, for the stone can restore the Dark Lord's shade to life.

You face new charges but others have heard the killer confess.

The Road Back: This, not the ordeal, is really the black moment of the book. What is the black moment, you ask? Ah—good question. It's the point in the story when the protagonist's goal seems unattainable, the conflicts unresolvable. She or he may even face death in pursuit of the quest.

Luke and his comrades-in-arms struggle to destroy the Death Star. Harry and his friends drop through the trapdoor. They encounter and pass several magical tests before Harry meets Quirrell and Voldemort. Harry magically finds the Philosopher's Stone in his pocket, but nearly dies in the struggle to keep it from Voldemort.

You are tried for multiple murder.

Resurrection: Also called the climax. Luke gains the confidence in himself he needs, switches off his fighter's weapons targeting mechanism, and blows up the Death Star. Harry survives due to his mother's sacrifice.

You and your attorney win your trial.

Return with the Elixir: With his newfound self-assurance, Luke has saved the rebellion and is rewarded. Harry defeats Voldemort, preventing him from using the Philosopher's Stone to reanimate.

You are again free, but with a new love of liberty. You have been transformed by the experience into a wiser person.

Legacy from the Distant Past

I wrote earlier that this story is hardwired into our consciousness, our bodies, our very cells. Why?

Picture this:

We are asleep in a cave or a den, curled up with our mates, our brothers, our sisters. This is our ordinary world.

Dawn comes, sliding sly fingers into the darkness. We awaken. Hunger and thirst are our call to adventure. Is there a refusal of the call to join the hunt? Perhaps from some pack members—the old, the very young, nursing mothers.

But others are insistent, approaching the alpha of the pack—the mentor—with a demand for food. Those who answer the call leave the safety of the cave—crossing the threshold.

The alpha selects our best fighters, finding allies while rejecting enemies who might take an opportunity to betray him during the excitement—the test—of the hunt.

We form a hunting party and set forth, seeking prey. But our targets are wily and fast. Some may take refuge in a different cave, behind a waterfall, or in a swamp.

Nevertheless, the alpha leads us to the danger, for the pack must eat. This stage of the hunt corresponds to Campbell's approach to the innermost cave.

We find another dire wolf trying to kill a great beast, perhaps a mastodon. Even the combined efforts of the pack with our new ally aren't equal to taking the mastodon, which tramples off, dripping blood from wounds we have inflicted. However, we have gained a powerful new hunter. These events are the ordeal and the reward.

We are not discouraged. After a rest, we track the mastodon, running through woodland and meadow, snouts on the ground to scent its blood trail. We know that the beast must be weary and weakened from the first battle. We are determined to bring it down and feed our family.

We find and corner the wounded animal, but it continues to fight fiercely. Its sharp tusks are vicious weapons. Our alpha is slashed brutally along one side. His guts spill out and he dies.

We are losing. The pack will not eat. Our family will not survive. This is the black moment, the road back.

The tide of the battle is turned when the new dire wolf takes leadership of the hunting party and brings down the mastodon—the resurrection.

The triumphant pack returns with the elixir, in this story the mastodon meat to feed the rest of the pack.

Because hunting is linked to survival, this basic quest structure is hardwired into each living creature, humans included.

Something that distinguishes humans from other creatures is that we invent and tell stories. The hunt is so closely tied to our survival that it makes sense that it would form the basis for the vast majority of our stories. That the object of the hunt may be a mastodon meal, the Holy Grail, or true love, is of little moment. Each story is one and the same: the story of the hunt.

An Alternative Strategy: The Four Act Structure

The four act structure I employ uses many of the quest elements identified by Campbell and Vogler, but I believe mine is simpler to understand and easier to use. And in our fast-paced, modern society, many of the traditional hero's journey elements are compressed into the same scene, are transposed, or are harder to find.

Act One: Conflict—the call to adventure—is introduced within the hero's ordinary world. Also in these scenes, the inner conflicts of the protagonist (or protagonists, in a romance or a longer, more complex book) must be shown to the reader.

Most often, the call to adventure will begin an outer conflict. The hero's inner conflicts will become evident as he grapples with the problem he's encountered—in Campbell's parlance, he crosses the threshold—as the inner conflicts will block him or her from solving the mystery or meeting the challenge.

All of this helps the writer define the major characters and their personalities. Describing the ordinary world fulfills two purposes. First, character is rounded and amplified.

Second, setting is described. Setting is often ignored by unskilled or newbie writers, but it is as crucial as

[33]

character or conflict. Indeed, some settings are so powerful that they function as characters. Hogwarts School, which alters its conformation as needs arise, is a perfect example.

Worth noting is the use of setting to heighten emotion, which can be accomplished in a variety of ways. We can use an exciting or interesting setting to increase the intensity of a reader's reaction to a scene. In fact, using setting to increase dread is so common in horror films that a scene in a graveyard or a crumbling mansion has become such a cliché that writers and filmmakers often avoid those settings as overused.

Or, we can place a scene in a mundane location and contrast that with highly dramatic events.

Early in *The Fisher King* (the 1991 film, not the legend), the protagonist has met his adored wife in a bar after work—an ordinary event in his ordinary world. The bar is full of chatting, happy folk, the mood is upbeat and the couple, delighted to see each other, are clearly in love. Then the woman's head is blown away by a shotgun-wielding mass murderer. The contrast between the commonplace but cheerful scene and the brutal killing shocks the viewer. Its impact on me was so severe that I have never watched that film again since it initially came out.

The message? Don't miss a chance to heighten emotion in whatever way you can. Don't skip setting each of your scenes effectively, both to transmit information about your characters and to heighten reader emotions.

But you don't need and shouldn't give the reader too much about setting at once. In our highly interconnected world, we can use shared cultural norms and information. For example, if I set a scene in a Starbucks or similar shop, I don't have to provide too much description, because the vast majority of my readers have bought coffee in such a place. A couple of phrases will suffice—readers will use their imaginations and their memories to supply the details. If there's anything that you need to feature to make your story work, or course you have to mention it, but otherwise, don't slow the pacing down by inserting a lot of unnecessary specifics.

When your now well-described hero embarks upon his quest, he will soon encounter some setback or unexpected event that may throw the story into a different, exciting direction. This is sometimes called a turning point or plot twist and is the end of Act One.

Here are a couple of examples: In the beloved children's classic, *Charlotte's Web,* Wilbur the pig, beloved pet of Fern the farm girl, moves from his home to the farm of Fern's Uncle Homer. His ordinary world of the farm, his companions there, and the pattern of his days are described. At the end of Act One, he meets Charlotte A. Cavatica, a spider.

In this short children's book, conflicts are simple. Even the youngest reader knows that Wilbur's probable fate is becoming pork chops and bacon, even if our piglet hero isn't yet aware of this. Toward the end of Act One, his loneliness brings Charlotte to the rescue, and his initial, mild inner conflict is solved.

[35]

The film *Titanic* has more characters with more complexities and therefore more complex and interesting conflicts. Thus, it's a more complex story, simplified here to show its well-structured plot.

Titanic is told in flashback through the memories of Rose, shown at the beginning of the film as an elderly woman telling her story to treasure-hunters searching the wreck for a valuable gem.

However, when the *Titanic* first leaves port on its maiden voyage, she's a well-born young woman dreading the arranged marriage that would solve her family's financial problems. Desperate, she contemplates suicide while alone at the ship's stern. Jack Dawson, an impoverished young artist, convinces her not to jump. When the couple is discovered by others, including her fiancé, Rose says that Jack saved her from falling over the ship's side.

A number of conflicts are evident. Rose's internal conflict is, "Should I or not? Should I wed as planned, or should I choose a less predictable life with Jack?" Dovetailing with this issue is an external conflict often found in many a romance—a couple is kept apart due to economic class differences, a man against society conflict. But the film's most significant external conflict, man against nature, isn't overtly stated. It doesn't need to be, because just about every viewer, even the most ignorant, is aware of the most famous sea disaster in history. We are merely shown the wreck on the ocean floor.

Act Two: At this point in your story, the hero or heroes should be further defined along with inner and outer conflicts. As you write, you should keep in mind that you

[36]

are proceeding toward the midpoint of your story.

Midpoints are important. Consider the phenomenon of the "saggy middle," the part of the story that can become dull or repetitive. In a romance novel, this will often manifest as a series of scenes that show the hero and the heroine being alternately attracted and repelled by each other. Unless the scenes are part of their journey to love, and exhibit realistic rather than contrived conflicts, they will become tedious.

In a mystery, your sleuths or sleuth will encounter events or phenomena which are clues to finding the killer or discovering the buried treasure—whatever it is your detectives seek. Some will be red herrings, and your job is to keep the quest interesting.

Many employ a three-act structure, combining Acts Two and Three into one. I cut them apart due to the threat of the saggy middle. When a writer keeps in mind that Act Two ends at the midpoint where something dramatic should happen, repetitiveness and boredom are avoided.

Along the way to the midpoint, your hero will meet allies and clash with enemies—but often s/he can't tell the difference. They may or may not meet a mentor. In my not-very-humble opinion, neither mentors nor allies are always necessary for a good story. Hemingway's *Old Man and the Sea* is pretty simple—just Santiago and a fish, with a teenager thrown in here and there. Not much in the way of mentors or allies in the middle of the Gulf Stream in this classic man against nature tale. Remember, the framework I'm discussing may not apply to literary fiction, which Hemingway's tale surely is.

[37]

However, allies, mentors, and enemies are useful to the author writing pop or genre fiction. Events must occur that propel the hero along his journey, and most realistic characters have friends, confidantes and enemies—just the way we do in our lives. Showing the protagonist with friends and enemies humanizes him or her, ensuring the character is likable and relatable.

In constructing Act Two your major task is to build dramatic tension before creating a strong midpoint. Use your tools—character and conflict—to develop the suspense that will energize your story. Tracing the growth of the conflicts is especially important here; the conflicts should explode at the midpoint. In the mythic structure, this is the approach to the innermost cave followed by the ordeal, which is the midpoint.

Your midpoint, which should be a powerful, exciting scene, will mark the end of Act Two. In many romance novels, the midpoint will be the first kiss or the first lovemaking when the attraction between your dual protagonists overcomes their conflicts—at least temporarily. In a mystery, another crime may take place or a major clue uncovered. In a thriller, the hero or heroes may encounter the villain for the first time, often barely escaping his clutches.

The best midpoint I've encountered lately is *Harry Potter and the Goblet of Fire.* Yep, you read that right—the whole book. Consider that Rowling created story arcs for each of the seven books in the series, but the series itself has a story arc or plot. *Goblet of Fire*, book number four out of seven, is the middle of the series and includes the dramatic event both characters and readers have been dreading: Voldemort's resurrection.

In *Charlotte's Web,* an elderly sheep tells Wilbur that he will be slaughtered in the autumn—man (or pig) against man. Now aware of his probable fate, Wilbur is in despair. He consults his friend Charlotte, who builds the words SOME PIG into her web, garnering human attention and praise for Wilbur. That unexpected midpoint prevents a saggy middle. As pleasant as this farmyard tale is, the story wouldn't interest us if Wilbur spent all his days sleeping in the sun and devouring the contents of his trough.

Aboard the *Titanic*, we find Rose and Jack's relationship deepening which, understandably, angers the fiancé. He and his manservant shadow and pursue the couple, trying to keep them apart. Nevertheless, their bond strengthens. The conflicts between the characters build toward confrontations that are interrupted by the ship hitting an iceberg, which rips open several of its compartments.

Act Three should build slowly but surely toward the black moment—when all may be lost—and the climax, when conflicts are resolved and the protagonist triumphs. This act may be longer than one-quarter of the book, because Act Four consists mostly of denouement.

In Act Three, conflicts are further defined and heightened. Lines are drawn. Enemies and allies choose sides, and the conflicts clarify until, at the black moment, they are stark.

A mystery's black moment will find the antagonist

confronting the protagonist, and the climax will see resolution of the conflicts and defeat of the enemy. In a romance, the protagonists will face their emotions and find their way to a lasting, loving relationship.

Act Three finds Wilbur, Charlotte and their human friends heading for the county fair. Though Charlotte is feeling her age, she manages to build Wilbur another web, this one with HUMBLE woven in the center. Later that night she constructs what she calls her magnum opus: her egg sac, filled with 514 eggs.

Wilbur and his friends are concerned about the pig in the sty next to his—that pig is much larger, and they fear that if Wilbur doesn't win a prize, he'll be slaughtered. The next day, the larger pig wins a blue ribbon. A frightened Wilbur relaxes only when he and his humans are given a special award. This is Charlotte's hour of triumph, when she knows that her friend's safety is assured.

But the opposite is not true. Wilbur loses his best friend when Charlotte dies of old age. However, the egg sac— Charlotte's legacy—travels with him back to the farm.

The *Titanic* is sinking. Everyone on board is initially disbelieving, then panicked (man against nature conflict). The fiancé's manservant has planted a piece of jewelry in Jack's pocket. When it's discovered, Jack is accused of theft and handcuffed to a pipe while the ship is going down (man against man). Rose rescues him and the two eventually end up in the water, clinging to a wooden door that is buoyant enough only for one. Jack heroically ensures Rose's survival but dies of hypothermia in the icy seas.

[40]

Act Four is the denouement, in which the tattered strings of the tale are neatly tied off. This would correspond to "Return with the Elixir" in the mythic story structure.

While the denouement may seem superfluous, it is not. Readers expect and want a last scene to wrap everything up and tie it in a tidy bow. When this doesn't take place, readers will complain. Trust me—I've made this error and been thoroughly lambasted for it.

The elixir in *Charlotte's Web* is her children. Though most take flight, using new, tiny webs as balloons to ride the wind, three stay with Wilbur. Author E.B. White then does a nice job describing the joys of Wilbur's life. Though several of Charlotte's progeny always stayed with him, he never forgot his best friend.

In *Titanic,* a rescued Rose evades her family and her fiancé. She calls herself Rose Dawson to honor Jack, their love, and his sacrifice. Having been invested with his courage and spirit of adventure, she creates a rich, full life for herself.

GOOD AND BAD BEGINNINGS

How to start your book

Writing a book starts long before you open your new journal, or begin a new document on your computer and type "Chapter One." You need to have read a lot of books, and I don't mean craft works like this manual. Read, but not just anything.

Aspiring writers are often told, "read in your genre." But Faulkner said, "Read, read, read. Read everything—trash, classics, good and bad, and see how they do it. Just like a carpenter who works as an apprentice and studies the master. Read! You'll absorb it. Then write. If it's good, you'll find out. If it's not, throw it out of the window."

I don't completely agree with the above advice. Mine is: *Read well-written books.*

What books are they? Try using the internet to search for lists of the best books ever written in English, or whatever language in which you're planning to write. Do not read translated books. While many are great, you want to read excellent books by those who have mastered all aspects of writing. Book translators possess extremely refined skills, and writing an original work from start to "the end" is not often among them.

Be selective. While reading works such as *Sir Gawain and the Green Knight* in the original middle English may be interesting and educational, you want to read books that are written in the version of English we use, so as to accustom your ear and your mind to modern, grammatically correct language.

Exceptions are the King James Bible and just about anything written by William Shakespeare. These should sit at the top of your reading list as they're probably the most influential works written in the English language.

In her excellent writing manual, *Starting from Scratch,* Rita Mae Brown provides a lengthy list of very good books. Same with Stephen King in *On Writing,* though his list is (blessedly) shorter, and is more individual—he describes his list as "the best books I've read over the last three or four years." (Brown's list starts with *Caedmon's Hymn,* a poem from about 665 A.D., and ends with Anthony Burgess's *Earthly Powers,* 1981).

The purpose of extensive reading is not to entertain but to enlighten. Pay attention to what you're reading. Read books that call to you more than once, to figure out why they're compelling. Look at the big picture aspects first: character and conflict, plot and story. During the next reading you can analyze narrower mechanical concerns such as word choice and sentence structure. Ask yourself, "How does this writer use these tools to elicit a particular reaction from the reader?"

[43]

Third reading: start looking for subtleties such as symbolism, subtext, and theme. How does the writer express these? What images does the author employ? What words does she choose? How long or short are sentences, paragraphs, chapters? Why?

It's not the purpose of this treatise to teach everything there is to know about every aspect of fiction writing. It's not possible. But reading programs your brain in particular ways. I emphasize reading modern works, works that use the same sentence structure, grammar, and vocabulary common in contemporary fiction. Read to increase your knowledge of, and command over, your tools: words, sentences, paragraphs, scenes. Read great books over and over again. Learn an appreciation for the English language and good writing, even down to correct apostrophe placement and comma usage.

Reading well-written books will imprint strong storytelling, correct grammar, and good sentence structure upon your mind, and it's a lot easier to learn by reading than by taking classes. A lifetime of good reading can create a good writer. You'll become a more able author, especially if you're writing as well as reading, such as keeping a journal or making notes. It doesn't really matter what you're writing at this phase. If you're writing fiction, great. If not, that's okay too.

All of this is to encourage becoming thoroughly fluent in the English language. If you aren't, the sad truth is that you needn't try to write anything more complex than a shopping list or a thank-you note. Readers know what good writing is and isn't, and they can be as unforgiving about sloppiness as the plastic surgeon's patient.

You may also wish to take a class or two or five on writing and to attend workshops. Most of us continue to do so even after we've written many published books. As Stephen Covey recommends, "sharpen the saw."

When you've found the urge to put pen to paper or fingers to keyboard, where to start?

Most of us begin at the beginning. But even before you write that first word, an essential decision must be made: Who's going to tell your story?

Point of View (POV)

Many newbie writers have an unreasonably difficult time with this concept, but it's really simple. POV is just that— the point of view from which the story is related. The writer tells the story through the perception of one of the characters she's created, usually the protagonist. *Alice's Adventures in Wonderland* is a perfect example. Everything in Wonderland is seen through Alice's eyes. Likewise, Bilbo Baggins. In *The Hobbit*, Tolkien almost always uses Bilbo as his point of view character, that is, telling his story from his point of view, relating his perceptions.

What's important to understand, and key to selecting the point of view character and the type of POV, is that *the reader's information about what's going on in the story is limited by the perceptions of the point of view character.*

[45]

In other words, if your POV character wasn't in the room when, say, a murder took place, s/he didn't see it—which creates the mystery.

In popular fiction, we utilize few types of POV. There are only two at this time:

First person singular, in which we are entirely and always within the mind of a single POV character. Here's an example of first person prose, possibly the most famous "cute first meet" ever written:

...we turned down a narrow lane and passed through a small side-door, which opened into a wing of the great hospital. It was familiar ground to me, and I needed no guiding as we ascended the bleak stone staircase and made our way down the long corridor with its vista of whitewashed wall and dun-coloured doors. Near the farther end a low arched passage branched away from it and led to the chemical laboratory.

This was a lofty chamber, lined and littered with countless bottles. Broad, low tables were scattered about, which bristled with retorts, test-tubes, and little Bunsen lamps, with their blue flickering flames. There was only one student in the room, who was bending over a distant table absorbed in his work. At the sound of our steps he glanced round and sprang to his feet with a cry of pleasure. "I've found it! I've found it," he shouted to my companion, running toward us with a test-tube in his hand. "I have found a re-agent which is precipitated by haemoglobin, and by nothing else. Had he discovered a gold mine, greater delight could not have shone upon his features.

[46]

"Dr. Watson, Mr. Sherlock Holmes," said Stamford, introducing us.

"How are you?" he said cordially, gripping my hand with a strength for which I should hardly have given him credit. "You have been in Afghanistan, I perceive."

"How on earth did you know that?" I asked in astonishment.

"Never mind," said he, chuckling to himself.
(from Doyle's *A Study in Scarlet*, 1887)

The easiest way to learn POV is to write a story using first person singular, like the above selection. The reader is always within the mind of the POV character, and if that character can't perceive an event taking place, that event can't be in the story. If the information is essential, you'll have to figure out another way of communicating it to the reader. There are a variety of ways to do this. Your protagonist may be told the info by another character. She may read an email, watch a TV show or psychically receive a message from beyond—whatever your fertile imagination can invent.

Consider carefully whether the reader actually needs that "essential" information. A piece of very good advice given in Browne and King's *Self-Editing for Fiction Writers* is "resist the urge to explain." Readers are smart. Plus, they need less information than most writers think to understand the characters and enjoy the book. In *On Writing*, Stephen King stated that he believes that a lot of bad writing is due to fear—we're afraid that the reader won't get it, so we overwrite. We don't have to give readers every snippet of data we know about our

[47]

characters, nor should we. We will always know more about them than will our readers, because much of what we know isn't relevant to the story and therefore shouldn't show up in the manuscript.

First person POV is wonderful for creating intimacy between the reader and the protagonist, so it's an exciting way to write a romance. It's also great for mysteries—the sleuth's information and ability to catch the crook are naturally restricted, heightening dramatic tension.

Third person limited is probably the most popular way we write fiction today. Again the story is shown from one character's viewpoint, but that viewpoint character can change. Other parts of the story may be told from the viewpoint of another character. This is called "multiple points of view." So another choice that the author confronts is determining from which character's viewpoint a particular scene is shown.

I use the phrase "a particular scene" because multiple points of view in the same scene are discouraged. This is commonly called *head-hopping,* and the conventional wisdom is that it annoys or even confuses the reader. Whether that's true is debatable, but what isn't debatable is that no good editor will allow head-hopping to sneak past her. And few reviewers or critics are likely to approve. However, it's generally okay for one POV change in a scene.

Here's an example of prose written in third person limited with a POV switch in the scene's middle. It's from a short story I wrote, *Lovers in Tartan*, which I'm using because of my familiarity with it, not because I want to sell more

[48]

copies. And I avoid copyright issues.

Edgar caught up with Isobel and Ranger in the forest. The horse now ambled rather than raced, the trees bordering the meadow surrounding the castle having slowed his flight. Edgar eased Dash into a walk and splashed through a brook while watching Ranger manage Isobel.

The stallion had apparently decided that he would no longer tolerate even Isobel's light weight, and proceeded to use a low-hanging branch to scrape her off. She landed flat on her back with a grunt. Ranger headed toward the stream and the new green grass beside it, thank the gods, instead of trampling the silly wench under his hooves.

Her laughter could be heard even from several yards away. "La! What a ride! I'll tame that mount yet." She sat up and rubbed her back.

Still on horseback, Edgar towered over her. "The only mount who needs taming is you. No harm done, milady?" He was pleased that he kept a mild tone of voice, because inside he was seething.

"None." She smiled up at him, her black eyes twinkling through the curtain of her lashes.

Bewitching, but he hardened his heart, determined that he'd not be led by the nose. He didn't like managing females, and if he allowed her to rule him now, she'd rule him forever. "Whatever possessed you to steal Ranger?"

"I didn't steal Ranger. I borrowed him."

[49]

"Against my express wishes. If your clumsiness has harmed him, Isobel—"

"My clumsiness?" She leaped to her feet.

He gave her a long, cool stare before turning away. He chirruped to Ranger, who raised his head from the sweet grass by the stream. Still chewing, he walked sedately to Edgar.

He dismounted to caress his horse's forehead before running his hands along the neck and body. Something hot and red billowed in Isobel's chest. What was it? 'Twas the same uncomfortable feeling she got when her younger brothers or sisters claimed too much of their parents' attention. The same horrible emotion that overcame her when other lassies dared to flirt with Edgar...which happened more frequently than she liked.

Jealousy.

She was jealous of the attention Edgar was giving to a horse. A horse.

Bloody hell.

The rest of the scene is written in Isobel's point of view—in other words, no head-hopping. No bouncing back and forth between Edgar's POV and Isobel's. Third person limited can be very intimate—we surely do understand Isobel's jealousy. And this POV is handy. We can know precisely what Edgar is thinking and what Isobel is feeling within the same scene, practically at the same time.

Here's an example of head-hopping—decide for yourself if you enjoy the selection.

*Upon entering the Starbucks, Jenna saw that Rachel's new hair stylist liked red. **Really** liked red, for Rachel's hair, formerly a sedate shade of ash blonde, was now closer to burgundy than chardonnay.*

"What do you think?" Rachel ran manicured fingers through her newly tinted locks. She was wearing a halter top that left her back bare, and she enjoyed the swish of her long mane against her naked skin.

Bill had followed his wife into the coffee shop. "Wild, baby," he commented. Jenna turned toward him, her eyes wide. He figured that maybe he shouldn't have sounded as though he was attracted to Rachel. Because he wasn't, was he? He loved Jenna. Had since the first moment they'd met.

This is pretty bad writing, deliberately so, but I hope you get the drift and understand why many find head-hopping undesirable.

In the past, **third person omniscient** point of view was common, far more so than it is now. The prefix *omni* originates in Latin and means *everything* or *all*. So, third person omniscient point of view can include everything. Using it, you're not limited at all, but can give a reader a godlike viewpoint. It's useful for providing information that isn't particular to an individual, information that can't be easily perceived or transmitted via a single character or even a couple of characters easily or conveniently.

The very famous opening of Dickens' *Tale of Two Cities* is a good example:

It was the best of times,
it was the worst of times,
it was the age of wisdom,
it was the age of foolishness,
it was the epoch of belief,
it was the epoch of incredulity,
it was the season of Light,
it was the season of Darkness,
it was the spring of hope,
it was the winter of despair,
we had everything before us,
we had nothing before us,
we were all going direct to Heaven,
we were all going direct the other way—

in short, the period was so far like the present period, that some of its noisiest authorities insisted on its being received, for good or for evil, in the superlative degree of comparison only.

There were a king with a large jaw and a queen with a plain face, on the throne of England;
there were a king with a large jaw and a queen with a fair face, on the throne of France.

In both countries it was clearer than crystal to the lords of the State preserves of loaves and fishes, that things in general were settled for ever.

It was the year of Our Lord one thousand seven hundred and seventy-five.

There are fashions in writing, just as there are in shoes and skirts. These days, the fashion in writing is in favor of intimacy, rather than distance, to draw the reader into the story. Third person omniscient is great for giving the reader a broad overview of the world in which a book is set, but bad for getting inside a character's head and heart.

Furthermore, the nineteenth century was a slower-paced time, and literature was slower-paced to match. Nevertheless, Dickens does not linger long in omniscient POV before he focuses upon one of the many fascinating folk he created in this novel.

Not only do you have to select the type of POV, but you must pick a POV character. We usually choose a character who's central to the action in the entire story and stick with that person—or persons, in the case of a romance—throughout, with few deviations.

We want to watch this central character meet and overcome her obstacles, becoming a better person thereby. Ideally, we live this growth and change with that character, learning something through the experience of reading the book.

If you choose first person limited, again: be aware that the reader will experience the story only from that character's perceptions. You have to decide if that approach will serve your story. In my mind, that means careful consideration

[53]

of whether the story I'm telling needs the intimacy that this POV affords. Another factor is whether this POV will overly limit what I can relate to the reader.

As I've indicated, often a romance or a mystery will benefit from this limited viewpoint, heightening the emotions undergone by the POV character and therefore intensifying the reader's experience when she or he lives the joy of falling in love or the terror of pursuit by a killer. Diane Farr points out that young adult literature—books directed toward teenagers—are often written in first person limited POV, mirroring teenagers' intensity and focus on their internal world.

Alternatively, you can heighten dramatic tension by using third person limited. If well-written, this POV can be just as intimate—maybe more so, because you can peek into the mind of more than one character and relate his or her experience to the reader, thus involving the reader emotionally with several of the personalities you've created. In a romance, the reader can experience falling in love from the viewpoint of both partners—or maybe all of them, in the case of a ménage tale.

And in a thriller, you can step into the thoughts of your villain. If you're writing, say, a serial killer book, that can be very chilling.

He turned the tap counterclockwise. After waiting a couple of minutes for the water to heat, he stepped into the oversized shower. He admired its custom glass-block construction and four shower heads, which rinsed the blood from his body quickly and efficiently.

He preferred to kill naked. Blood-soaked garments were a disposal problem and, if found, easily traceable evidence.

Though he avoided ruining good clothes, getting blood out from under his fingernails was a bitch.
(from *Deadly Waters, 2019*)

Thrillers are often written with third person limited for exactly this reason. In a thriller, the reader often knows who the antagonist is while the protagonist does not. The reader can then see the main characters, hero and villain, as they pursue each other. Watching the hero edge toward and then fall into the trap the villain has created raises the stakes, heightens the suspense, and draws the reader into the emotions, the dread, that the characters are experiencing.

Often a writer will choose the character who has the most at risk as the point of view character because of the powerful emotions that character is feeling, most often fear. Fear is the most basic of human emotions, and candidly, good writers spend a lot of time and words using and manipulating the fears of readers.

The first sentence

Stephen King once said, "An opening line should invite the reader to begin the story. It should say: Listen. Come in here. You want to know about this." He emphasized the importance of the first line reflecting the author's style, and gave the following as an example:

[55]

They threw me off the hay truck about noon.

In *The Postman Always Rings Twice,* James M. Cain's style and voice are spare, even elegant despite the folksy tone of the sentence. No useless words clog this sentence; most of us would have written "at about noon" rather than "about noon." And the line draws the reader in by providing intrigue about the narrator. As King points out, no one travels via hay truck willingly, so our protagonist is a drifter. The reader will want to know, "Who is this guy? What's he doing on a hay truck? Who threw him off and why?" and the most crucial question: "What's gonna happen next?"

So, your first sentence must hook the reader into wondering "Who's this person? What's up with him or her? What's gonna happen next?"

We can look at one of Stephen King's first lines (from *The Gunslinger*) as a fine example:

The Man in Black fled across the desert, and the Gunslinger followed.

We want to know who these people are and the reason one is trailing the other. We immediately get an impression of the characters—the Man in Black is fleeing, which implies speed and fear, but the Gunslinger is following. He's not chasing or pursuing. The choice of "following" implies a calm but determined hunt. And King gives us a little about setting, which immediately piques our curiosity. "What desert? Where?"

[56]

King has said that he will take months, even years, to evolve the right first sentence.

Here's one more example, and in this book the author starts with description. But the first sentence of *Harry Potter and the Philosopher's Stone* is not nearly as important as the chapter title that precedes it: *The Boy Who Lived.* In this book the chapter title substitutes for a first line most admirably. It promptly raises questions— "Who is this Boy? Why is it so special that he lived? Aren't most boys we read about alive?"

We're hooked. We want to know about this boy. And we read on.

How *not* to start your book

Your first scene—in fact, your first sentence—in any book are the most important words you'll ever write. Apart from the cover, this one sentence will sell your book to a reader.

Or not. A potential buyer may leave your book on the shelf or, in many cases, click his or her mouse and go to another writer's website to buy her books rather than yours.

How can you prevent this? How can you keep that reader at your site, buying and reading *your* books?

There's only one way: ***don't be boring.***

Don't start a book with the hero or heroine waking up and thinking about his or her predicament. You may think

[57]

you're hooking the reader but you're not, because *nothing is happening.* This is what we call an info dump. I discuss them more in *Write This, Not That!,* but what you need to always keep in mind is that they're deadly. They will kill your book before it starts.

Do not start with the protagonist on a journey, whether it be a plane flight, boat ride or train travel while thinking about (you guessed it) his or her predicament. And even if your hero or heroine is traveling to someplace cool, don't do this. It's almost as boring as starting your book with the protagonist asleep. All you're doing is providing another info dump.

The writer Elmore Leonard advised to never start a book with weather and to avoid prologues. I agree with the first rule—weather is generally dull—but not with the second. Prologues can be used to provide the reader with info s/he will need to enjoy the story. As long as the author observes the maxim "show, don't tell," prologues are okay.

Whether your first sentence begins your prologue or your first chapter, *start with action or dialog*. Start with something fun, evil, dramatic or just plain interesting.

Let's look at some examples, both good and bad. Possibly the most famous bad beginning was written by Edward Bulwer-Lytton:

It was a dark and stormy night.

Why is this a bad first sentence? First, the use of "it was" really irks, as those words weigh down the sentence and contribute nothing. The word "dark," likewise—aren't all nights dark? So we're left with "a stormy night" which isn't a sentence. The author is ineptly striving for drama using the setting rather than the characters and their conflicts, and the drama in any story should, most often, stem from the characters and their conflicts.

But then we have:

It was a dark and stormy night.

In her attic bedroom Margaret Murry, wrapped in an old patchwork quilt, sat on the foot of her bed and watched the trees tossing in the frenzied lashing of the wind. Behind the trees clouds scudded frantically across the sky. Every few moments the moon ripped through them, creating wraithlike shadows that raced along the ground.

Madeline L'Engle surely knew she was using one of the most famous clichés in literature to begin her ground-breaking young adult novel, *A Wrinkle in Time*. Clever writers may use subtle mockery to keep astute readers engaged. *A Wrinkle in Time* is proof that you can break the rules if you know what you are doing—but don't decide that you know what you're doing too early in your writing career.

A newbie mistake is to start the book too early in the story. A great example would be my first published novel, currently available in both paperback and digital formats as *Lord Devere's Ward*.

It's a Regency-set romance, and the original version

[59]

started with what I thought of as the inciting incident: the death of the heroine's grandfather, her guardian. I wrote it a number of years ago, and I can't find the original manuscript. But I recall that in the initial drafts, the first sentence was something like:

The dying man's last breath rattled in his throat.

Given that it was written by a newbie, it's not bad. But it's not great. It was written from the heroine's point of view; given that she was losing her beloved grandfather, her rock in life since her parents' deaths, it's a tad remote. Would she have been thinking of her grandfather at that moment as "the dying man"? Not likely. And she'd be frightened and sad, neither of which is conveyed by the sentence.

Far worse, what followed was about a hundred pages describing the Regency way of death. We slogged our way through a muddy autumn journey from Somerset to Wiltshire, where the funeral and interment took place at the family seat, Badham Abbey. Then came the funeral and the reading of the will, which made Lord Devere of the book's title the heroine's legal guardian while the guardian of her person was her uncle. Her uncle schemed to marry the heroine to his son and thereby gain control of her money.

I enjoyed doing the research—that's one reason I love to write historicals—but showing off one's knowledge should be limited to term papers, textbooks and final exams. Fiction is not the place to be a smarty-pants. I ultimately realized that the true inciting incident was the imprisoned heroine's escape.

This is how the book now opens:

Badham Abbey, Wiltshire, England
January, 1820

"God, help me!"

The logline and the first sentence convey a lot. Without much chit-chat, I told the reader where and when the story starts, and that our frantic heroine is in peril.

The next paragraphs reinforce this impression:

Kate Scoville kicked and flailed her feet, struggling to grip the tower wall with her oversized boots. She whispered a hasty prayer in the chance that the Almighty paid attention to her small corner of His world. Wearing clumsy, borrowed gloves, she grasped the rope tied to the attic window and pushed her boots against the side of the tower, seeking purchase on the wall.

At last, her toes found a mortared joint between two massive blocks of stone. She breathed deeply until her racing pulse steadied. The chill air knifed her lungs. She could see her breath, small puffy clouds, when she exhaled.

She looked down and gulped. Three far stories below her, the slate roof of the abbey gleamed, pale and frosty in the moonlight.

Notice, please, that Kate is not sitting up in bed or in a carriage contemplating her predicament. She's in the midst of the action; the object of choosing this particular place in her life story is to immediately hook the reader.

The words you choose

Though we could discuss word choice forever, we can't. But let's take a short look at some useful concepts.

Most of us in this business find ourselves more than once staring at the blank page or monitor wondering which word comes next. When my writer's block has been severe, I haven't been able to choose between even *and, a, but,* or *when.*

But assuming you are pleasantly and productively unblocked, what words should you choose?

First, unless you're writing a treatise like this one, use short, direct words. In *Starting from Scratch,* Rita Mae Brown notes that the strongest and clearest words in our language are derived from Anglo-Saxon roots, while the more high-falutin' have Latin roots. She notes a number of what she calls "parallel words," that is, words with similar meanings but different origins. It's easy to note which are strong, Anglo-Saxon based words as opposed to the more elegant Latinate: woman and female, friendship and amity, help and aid are a few of the examples she gives (provides).

There are some exceptions to this rule, most notably in historical fiction. Regency romance, for example, uses a particular vocabulary which may include longer words that were popular at that time (roundaboutation, grumbletonian, and the like) as well as shorter slang terms that were knows as "cant." The language was rich but to the modern ear, full of obscurities—except to a fan of Regency fiction. Readers of that genre demand that somewhat stilted vocabulary. So observe the conventions of the genre or subgenre in which you write. This is not to say you can't go outside those conventions, but observe them, know what they are.

Note the sounds of the words you pick. While I hope that your fans do not move their lips while reading your work, I think that maybe everyone hears the words inside their minds while reading.

Consider this subtle and marvelous first sentence, from Daphne du Maurier's *Rebecca:*

Last night I dreamt I went to Manderley again.

What can we note about the words du Maurier used? First off, they're all short except the name of the place—Manderley. That name stands out, and should. As in any Gothic, the setting is crucially important in this novel, so important that it virtually functions as another character.

What else strikes us? How do these words sound?

They're soft and dreamy, reflecting the mood of the protagonist. No hard sounds at all. Du Maurier wants to take us back to a different time and place, the landscape of her protagonist's dream—or her nightmare, for the description turns frightening. Throughout the novel, Manderley is slowly revealed as a threat, not a haven.

Most of the novel is told in flashback, a device few authors are skilled enough to do well, but is foreshadowed by the dreaminess of the beginning.

Some words have sounds that more closely reflect their meaning. For example, contemplate the differences between *assail, assault,* and *attack.* All three have similar meanings. But *attack* is the better word to choose in most cases due to its strong consonants, which reinforce its meaning.

All three are verbs, words that describe action. Be choosy when picking these—and any other word—for it's easy to fall back upon derivatives of *to be.* While *was* is indispensable, it's also overused. Same with *felt, stepped, walked* or *went.* Try to find a word that's more descriptive.

"I went to the store" is okay, but "I sprinted to the store" gives the reader a little more, a sense of urgency. It piques the reader's interest (Why's she in such a hurry?). And "I rode to the store on the beautiful Arabian my parents gave me for my fourteenth birthday" says a lot, showing us that the character is from a wealthy family and is grateful for the birthday gift.

Don't miss a chance to infuse more meaning into even the most mundane act. "She strode to the operating table" says more about your surgeon than "she went", and "she staggered" gives us even more, though it might be unwelcome information to the hapless patient. English, a wonderfully descriptive and flexible language, has many verbs describing how we go from one place to another. Use them.

But don't overdo the exotic or weird word. In fact, don't use them at all. *Strode* or *staggered* are okay, but *perambulate*? No. First of all, there's no additional meaning to the word—it merely means that someone went. And it distracts from the story. Your tools exist to tell your story, and the instant that they distract or detract, you've blown it. Keep the reader entranced by your fascinating characters and dramatic action, not irritated by the use of obscure vocabulary that doesn't add anything.

Let's look again at the snippet I quoted from *Lord Devere's Ward*. Scroll back up there and note these verbs: *kicked, flailed, grasped, knifed.* Short, sharp verbs, with lots of strong consonants, suitable for describing a character in peril.

And in those paragraphs, what *don't* you see?

A single use of *to be* or any of its variants.

The words you pick help your characters tick

Often neglected is careful selection of the words we choose to express our characters' personalities. A farm laborer will speak differently than a banker. In fact, she will even think differently, from ideas to images and beyond.

Our characters' worldviews and personalities should be reflected in the way they think and speak. Consider who your character is when you choose the words to describe their thoughts and the words they utter. Scout, the

Alabama-born protagonist of *To Kill a Mockingbird*, will not think and speak like Katniss Everdeen of the Hunger Games trilogy. Both will use different words than Britisher Harry Potter, even though all three share similarities in that they're fairly young.

Word choice is an essential aspect of characterization. Oddly, though, I'll read book after book—many by very successful authors—in which one can't tell the difference between characters based on their thoughts and words. After a while, those books take on a dull sameness.

James Michener's ponderous style is immediately recognizable...

For if the old man who led them was practical, sitting on his ankles and working his flint to that richly satisfying moment when he could begin tapping with his small stone hammer, flaking off one sharp knife blade after another— he was still a spiritual man whose tired eyes could see beyond the desert to those invisible summits of the imagination where cool air existed and where the one god, El-Shaddai, lived.

(from *The Source*, 1965)

...even in a romantic scene:

He felt himself caught up in passions he had thought long dead, while the girl smiled softly to herself and, knowing she was the envy of all the others for her man could dance, thought, "I got the best one of the group and I was smart enough to ask for him."

(from *Hawaii*, 1959)

[66]

Conversely, John Steinbeck wrote in many different voices. The style in *Tortilla Flat* (1935) is distinctly different from that found in his 1976 *The Acts of King Arthur and his Noble Knights*—even though the subject matter is the same, *Tortilla Flat* being a retelling of the Arthurian fables through the eyes of California *paisanos.*

Here are two illustrative excerpts:

"I ask that you make me a knight," said Gawain.

"I will gladly," said Arthur. "You are my sister's son and I owe you every honor."

And:

The sergeant lined them up in front of his desk. They passed everything but the sobriety test and then the sergeant began his questions with Pilon.

"What branch do you want to go in?"

"I don' give a god-damn," said Pilon jauntily.

The mythic quality of the Arthurian legend contrasts with the forthright enjoyment of life that Steinbeck saw in the *paisanos.*

So the words we choose can express character as well as create an emotional reaction in the reader—best if you can do both at the same time, as in the snippet from *Tortilla Flat.*

[67]

SCENE AND SEQUEL, CHAPTERS AND PARAGRAPHS

Scenes are the building blocks of your story, for acts are comprised of scenes. They're nothing more than events, most often interactions between your characters. Scenes should fulfill at least one or two of the below purposes— try to include all four.

- Advance plot
- Reveal or develop character
- Complicate or resolve conflict
- Express setting, mood, theme

Everything in your manuscript should have a function, even every comma or em-dash. And this is the reason the special world we create in our stories is so different from our ordinary world. Much happens in our day-to-day existence isn't particularly relevant to the story of our lives, that is, the accomplishment of our dreams and goals.

Let's say that we're thinking of having our protagonist, who has as his goal great wealth, stop at a Chipotle restaurant for a burrito. Eating that burrito doesn't help accomplish that goal. But it's a common act, one that occurs often. Lunch is a part of our lives, but we wouldn't put it in a book about a protagonist on a quest to amass loads of money unless something occurred at that Chipotle that fulfills one or two of the above purposes.

Perhaps the protagonist meets someone there who is a mentor, ally or adversary; he could eat lunch with his hippie mom, who vehemently expresses her dismay over his life choices.

Maybe he heroically stops an armed robbery from taking place, garnering publicity that helps him on his way—even though he gives up the chance to close the biggest deal of his life, a sacrifice that would make his eventual triumph all the more poignant. And the event shows character, that this guy is more than a soulless money-making machine.

If he's just eating lunch, his burrito probably doesn't belong in your book. The scene might show a tiny bit about your character, but that's not enough to justify an entire scene. A short phrase (He devoured a burrito at Chipotle before heading back to the stock exchange—where he hoped to complete the biggest deal of his life) is all that's necessary.

So before you write an interaction or an event, you—as well as your characters—must have a goal. What's the scene for? What are you trying to show the reader about your characters?

Where are you in the plot? If this scene is early in the story, you're probably conveying character and setting to the reader as well as advancing conflict (rather than resolving it).

And, most importantly, **_don't be boring._** Readers are bombarded by stimuli, especially from the media. Your book must hold their attention not merely by being well-crafted but unusual, different in some way that adds to their experience.

Emotion is the key to drawing a reader into the special world you're creating, into the story, into the minds and hearts of your characters. And that's the key to starting your scene. Notice in the excerpt from *Lord Devere's Ward* that Kate's terror is immediately conveyed.

Each scene will have an arc similar to the structure of the entire novel, but simpler. All twelve elements need not be present in a scene, but generally, scenes build to a climax before the emotion tapers off.

That tapering, which is often comprised of introspection by the hero about what transpired in the scene, is sometimes called *sequel*. Events happen, and then the hero considers those events and their impact on his quest. Scene and sequel are similar to cause and effect, or action and reaction.

Scene structure is very like lovemaking, and a well-written love scene in a romance will illustrate the point. Foreplay is followed by the main action, then a climax. Afterglow corresponds to sequel or denouement, and a scene's sequel is as necessary as a novel's denouement.

After intense action, the reader needs an opportunity to draw his breath and allow his racing pulse to slow, especially in a thriller or suspense novel. But note that in our fast-paced culture, that sequel may be only a sentence or two.

In *Alice's Adventures in Wonderland,* Alice often encounters some creature or incident that's puzzling, after which she'll briefly consider what happened. One of the more famous quotes from the book is the sequel after her talk with the Cheshire Cat:

"Well! I've often seen a cat without a grin," thought Alice; "but a grin without a cat! It's the most curious thing I ever saw in all my life!"

Early in *The Final Problem*, Sherlock Holmes is pursued by Professor Moriarty, who nearly catches him at Victoria Station. A disguised Holmes eludes his nemesis and escapes London, leaving his enemy fuming on the platform. When he joins Watson on the train, here's the sequel:

"With all our precautions, you see that we have cut it rather fine," said Holmes, laughing. He rose, and throwing off the black cassock and hat which had formed his disguise, he packed them away in a hand-bag.

This paragraph is followed by more dialog, including the revelation that Moriarty had tried to kill Holmes by setting fire to his Baker Street flat. The conversation constitutes the sequel, substituting admirably for the introspection that often forms sequel. Using dialog is a good choice because interaction is almost always more interesting than introspection.

Sequel also has a structure, according to Jack M. Bickham, author of *Writing Novels that Sell* (1989). That linear structure is *emotion, quandary, decision, action.* The

[71]

character, after enduring whatever happened in the scene, comes down from his emotions and, in considering what has just happened, often realizes he is facing a quandary. Thinking about the situation results in a decision, which is followed by action.

Let's look again at the brief little story I made up to illustrate the mythic structure, examining it for the essentials of scene and sequel. In it, our hero awakens and stumbles into his kitchen to see his roommate dead on the floor. That's the scene. Awakening is the foreplay part of the scene. The main action and the climax are stumbling into the kitchen to see the dead roommate. The sequel is when, shocked, he realizes that the dead body presents him with a quandary—What should he do? He concludes he's hallucinating (decision) and crawls back into bed (action).

Another approach to writing a scene is to start in the middle of the action. The snippet I shared from *Lord Devere's Ward* is illustrative. The scene starts with Kate nearly falling to her death. Much happened to her before, but that information wasn't immediately necessary to tell her story. So I cut it, and started at the midpoint of the scene, inserting only bits of backstory here and there to make her situation understandable.

Her escape from the abbey is the climax. Then she makes her way to the road, while considering her predicament and wondering where she will find safety—the sequel.

In the manuscript I did not tell the reader directly what her decision and action were, but began the next scene in London, with Kate demanding entrance to Lord Devere's manse. Bickham stated, "...presenting the story in straight chronology often leads to a story that plods, is predictable, is too even and boring, and doesn't have the surprises and dramatic peaks that it otherwise might have." He also wrote, "A scene or sequel may be skipped entirely."

If you wish to read the entire scene, it can be found in one of the appendices. I urge you to do so, because you'll find that the material fulfills all four purposes indicated above.

In regard to the length of scenes: As a romance novelist, I tend to write long scenes because the essence of a romance, to me, is the interaction between the lovers. In my view, the longer the interaction, the better. A long scene gives the opportunity to show your characters grow and work through their conflicts to a lasting love. An exercise I set for myself is after I write a scene between my characters is to challenge myself to write one or two more pages of interaction—just to see what they'll do. This way I can write richer, deeper, more interesting interactions, scenes that expose and develop character more fully.

But scene length is a matter of personal style, and you will develop yours. What's important is that the scene has purpose, structure, and interest.

A brief word about chapters

Chapters do not partake of the same structural concerns we have about our story as a whole or our scenes. According to one online source, they may have evolved from the early practice of writing on papyrus, with chapter breaks occurring when the roll of papyrus ended.

A chapter break is a convenient place to begin a new scene, or to change the point of view in the scene you're writing. It may be the opportunity to leap forward in time, or at least to step or jump. Like lovemaking, the beginning of a chapter should be seductive and enticing. You must hook the reader.

You may begin with dialog, description, narration or action, whatever you prefer or whatever suits the story, but remember that description and narration are intrinsically less interesting than dialog and action. So, again—emphasize dialog and action in your story at all times.

I'm sure by now you've memorized my maxim, **don't be boring.** Your writing will become predictable if you always begin and end a chapter the same way. The novelist Dan Brown, the author of the *DaVinci Code*, has become so well-known for closing chapters on cliffhangers that it's almost a jest. (A cliffhanger, by the way, is a nifty shorthand way of saying, "a point of high suspense.")

But what he does makes sense, because a chapter break is an opportunity for your reader to put your book aside. Same with scene breaks. Your job as a writer is to motivate your reader to keep reading, and as I've said, there's only one way to do that—**don't be boring.**

However, you need not end every scene or chapter with a

cliffhanger to avoid a bored reader. If you did your job well, especially in the first few pages in the book, your reader should be so invested in your characters and their quest that she will read on even if your heroine is not facing disaster or death at every moment.

Chapter length is mutable. As I've mentioned, everything is subject to fashion and style, and right now the fashion is for short chapters. When I began writing back in the Dark Ages, longer chapters were preferred. Chapter length is a matter of your personal style and voice, which will evolve as you grow as a writer.

In other words: don't worry about it. Your reading of great works of literature should imbue you with an instinct for chapter length and content.

Paragraphs

For many, creating paragraphs in fiction—that is, dividing parts of a scene or interaction into manageable bits—is such an obvious process that it doesn't need discussion. (Non-fiction is completely different and beyond the scope of this treatise). In *Starting From Scratch,* Rita Mae Brown doesn't discuss paragraphs in fiction at all. I also had thought it was fairly easy until I encountered *Fifty Shades of Grey*, which contained selections like the following:

"Very well, Mr. Grey," she mutters, then exits. He frowns, and turns his attention back to me.

"Where were we, Ms. Steele?"

[75]

Oh, we're back to Ms. Steele now.

"Please, don't let me keep you from anything."

Normally, when we write interactions between people, the actions, words, and thoughts of each person are grouped in separate paragraphs. When we switch people, we create a new paragraph. So this selection should have been written thusly:

"Very well, Mr. Grey," she mutters, then exits.

He frowns, and turns his attention back to me. "Where were we, Ms. Steele?"

Oh, we're back to Ms. Steele now. "Please, don't let me keep you from anything."

What's the reason behind this convention? So the reader can know who's thinking and talking, we place the identifying dialog tag along with the dialog. Often we may not need a tag at all, when only two people are interacting. The convention makes this possible. Readers know that when a paragraph ends, the next paragraph belongs to another character.

Another author, Jennifer Crusie, runs the acts and words of two characters together for effect, as in this snippet from *Welcome to Temptation* (2000):

"Can I talk to you alone?" Phin said to Sophie, and she said, "Anyplace but a bedroom," so they went down to the dock.

[76]

I emailed both authors to ask about their paragraphing choices, and Crusie responded, "Normally it's one speaker per paragraph because that's the rhythm of normal, relaxed speech. But when people are tense, when they snap back or cut each other off, it's hard to reproduce that rhythm with two paragraphs because the white space between the paragraphs is always read as a pause. So if I want to create the illusion that the interchange is short and sharp or overlapping, I paragraph the two people together. It's grammatically incorrect, but it's the only way to get that rhythm."

That's not the usual way we create paragraphs in dialog, where the words and actions of each character merit their own paragraph. Jack Bickham calls this a "dialog package."

He also points out that dialog follows the structure of stimulus and response. His advice? When a stimulus is concluded, hit the return key, make a new paragraph and write the response. This is true for dialog as well as action and narrative.

You may wish to write short, snappy paragraphs to create a quicker pace, plus more movement and tension in your writing just as shorter sentences heighten pace and tension. Same with lines of dialog. Alternatively, longer sentences, paragraphs and lines of dialog will slow pacing. Use each for whatever dramatic effect you wish to achieve, but keep in mind that mixing it up is a good thing—vary the length of dialog, paragraphs, sentences. Remember: ***don't be boring.***

EPILOGUE

There's more, of course

As you learn more and develop your skills you will find yourself naturally drawn to using more advanced techniques. There are too many to list, but at that time I urge you to study concepts such as subtext, symbolism, myth, and theme.

Theme and voice are distantly related, as we often find ourselves unconsciously writing about the same theme over and over. For example, my books tend to be about women overcoming obstacles, growing, and discovering their personal power. That's my overarching theme, and it's popped into most if not all of my books without me really thinking about it.

That's part of my voice. An author's voice is the way she unconsciously chooses words, structures phrases, creates characters, plots stories. Newbie writers often worry that overzealous editors and critique partners will drain their voice out of their manuscripts. It's true that a manuscript can be over-edited, resulting in stilted prose, but voice is so basic that it can't be edited out, in the same way that theme is an aspect of storytelling that is intrinsic.

So that's about the only aspect of writing you don't have to worry about. The rest is up to you. You can give as much or as little of yourself to the writing as you choose. But as with many things in our world, the more you give, the more you get.

Good luck! And remember—***don't be boring.***

WRITE THIS, NOT THAT!

A while back I initiated an online discussion with some other writers about books. My question was: what earns a book a home in our hearts rather than a trip to the shredder? I gathered comments from several yahoo groups before adding them to the knowledge garnered from a lifetime of reading, sixteen years of fiction writing, and a mini-career editing for individuals as well as for a variety of publishing companies.

I have authored and edited most kinds of writing from academic treatises to the sexiest erotica. Although much of my experience is in romance, the principles I relate are applicable to most fiction.

Some information surprised me while other statements struck me as mundane. And I found startling omissions: for example, many didn't decry the lack of a happy ending in a few books, preferring an interesting ending to a predictable one. But many comments focused on a few well-defined topics: dialog and tags; the despised info dump; a category I call "respecting the language;" avoiding clichés, both verbal and situational; characterization errors; plotting missteps and a failure to edit. The "talking head in the empty room syndrome" is a particular irritant to me, and, as a former acquiring editor, I have strong opinions regarding synopses.

[81]

Many mistakes can and should be avoided or fixed before anyone, even a critique partner, sees your work in progress.

DIALOG, THE CORE OF YOUR NOVEL

Romances are all about the interactions between two people. In fact, most novels, unless they're Hemingway's *The Old Man and the Sea* or similar books, involve the interactions between people, and most of these interactions are verbal. But dialog can be especially tricky to write.

Here's what you can do: **Listen and cut.**

To avoid stilted dialog, listen. Go to different venues and eavesdrop. Coffee houses, like Starbucks and Peet's. Bars. Truck stops and grocery stores. If you write for the young adult market, go to where teens are. When you take your kid and her friends to a concert or to the opening of the next hot teen flick, don't drop them off and leave. Go in. Listen. Not to the concert but to the kids, not just yours but others.

If you're fortunate enough to travel, do the same research wherever you go. Don't stay in your hotel. Walk a few blocks away to a local café or dive and listen to the locals chat. Take notes. Focus on the words people use and the way they put sentences together. Note slang terms.

Have you ever noticed that in some parts of the USA people say soda rather than pop? In other American locales, any fizzy drink is a Coke, whether or not it's cola.

[83]

In Georgia, a woman's handbag is a pocketbook, even if the satchel can't fit into her pocket. In California it's her purse. Regional differences in speech are numerous and fascinating. Note them. Use them.

Listen, but cut

Many of my conversations run something like this:

"Hiya!"

"Hey, hi, Sue. How're ya doin'?"

"I'm okay. You?"

"Fine. Whassap?"

"Not much. Tryin' to stay dry."

The only variations are seasonal. In January, I'm trying to stay dry. In July, I'm trying to stay cool.

The conversation doesn't say much and I'd never put it in a book, unless I wanted to lull the reader into an unsuspecting stupor before a vampire sank fangs into a victim or a meteor slammed into our planet.

So the vast majority of realistic interactions don't belong in a book. Interactions should have a purpose; in fact, every word in your book should have a purpose.

What purposes can we define?

- Advance plot
- Develop character
- Complicate or resolve conflict
- Express setting, mood, theme.

Ideally, a line of dialog and its tag can fulfill more than one purpose. Here's an example from *Highland Vampire*, a short story I wrote in 2009:

We were awakened by screams splitting the early morning, followed by pounding on the gatehouse door.

"Mister Garrett! It's happened again!"

Garrett rolled over, smiled at me and said, "See?"

I blinked, trying to understand. "What?"

"Get up, sweetheart, the fun is just beginning." He was already out of bed, pulling on jeans and a moss green sweater that looked especially good with his eyes.

I followed suit, adding a denim jacket against the misty morning. "Do you know what's going on?"

He grinned. "It's the vampire. He's struck again."

Quite a bit happens during this snippet of dialog. Our hero and heroine awaken to a situation they must handle, so they dress with haste. There's a vampire whose intervention isn't entirely unwelcome. The story is advanced while conflict is indicated.

Their relationship appears to be a positive one. The heroine is confused, noticing her lover's sweater and eyes even though there's a crisis to be managed. This is a character note. Here's another character note: The hero, who's addressed as "Mister," is expected to deal with the vampire. So he's a leader, someone who's respected. However, he seems pleased that the vampire has struck again. Again, the plot is advanced, conflict is implied while emotion is communicated. Setting details—a gatehouse on a misty morning—are mentioned.

Dialog tags

Notice how most of the dialog tags are action tags. Action tags perform two functions. They indicate which character spoke while adding a little bit to the story.

Action tags are great. Action tags avoid the "talking head" problem, identified by Loucinda McGary when I solicited ideas for this article.

Action tags move the story along, showing mood or personality while your characters are talking to each other. If a character paces, scratches his head or smokes a cigarette while speaking, he's anxious. If she's mixing paints, cooking dinner or weightlifting, she's multi-tasking and therefore a bit distracted—perhaps the conversation isn't important to her, or she's busying her hands so as not to appear nervous.

Your hero and heroine may talk while in bed, while eating,

[86]

while walking together. These situations provide ample opportunity to write action tags, which insert emotion and story into the conversation.

Action tags also help avoid major but common missteps that can creep into dialog tags, such as the following:

> He growled.
> She snarled.
> He grunted.
> She hissed.

Unless your characters are were-animals, please don't use these tags or anything like them, or at least, not often. Once in a while, which means a handful of times in your manuscript—no more.

Avoid "he interrupted," "he responded," "she demanded" and the like. Your excellent dialog will tell the reader that the character is interrupting or responding to another. So the verbiage is unnecessary and does nothing but slow down the pacing.

With short attention spans so prevalent in our fast-moving culture, pacing in all media has sped up. Look at how quickly video games move. The action in films, likewise. Everything moves faster and your books should also.

At this point you might be asking yourself: "What about Suzie's writing? Do her characters growl, snarl or snap? Do they murmur or whisper?"

Sure they do. More often in earlier works, when I didn't know better. But not so much nowadays. So these dialog tags retain their effectiveness because I don't use them frequently. Plus, readers don't get the opportunity to become irritated by the incessant repetition of an intrusive dialog tag.

You may wonder, "Don't best-selling writers use these tags?" Yep, they sure do. If I had a nickel for every time a certain best-selling author has written "he rasped" I might never have to work again.

But these writers aren't popular because they use intrusive dialog tags, but despite this bad habit. They're successful because they're great storytellers (and for a plethora of other career-related reasons which aren't the subject of this article).

So, what dialog tags are okay?

> He said.
> She said.
> He asked.
> She asked.

And that's pretty much it.

As many commentators have stated, these dialog tags are all but invisible to the reader. You can also skip using any tag at all, but just when there are only two people in the conversation. Readers will understand who's talking by the form of the dialog, as I discussed in the section on paragraphs in *Plotting and Planning*. But that can't go on

[88]

for too long. Insert an action tag, or you'll end up with talking heads.

If you don't believe me, that's okay. You can consult one of the best craft books around, *Self Editing for Fiction Writers* by Browne and King, in which you'll read pretty much the same opinion as mine.

Additional missteps you need not make follow.

THE INFO DUMP

Rarely excusable or well-written, the info dump is often disguised as amusing dialog in an engaging scene. Seldom can info dumps be forgiven regardless of the cleverness or wit involved because they are intrinsically boring. They are often dull because they relate past events, generally to set up conflicts.

Conflicts are good (no conflict, no story, right?) but if backstory is necessary, weave it in or write a prologue, with the information in an action scene. In other words (and I know you've heard this before): *show, don't tell.*

Info dumps received frequent and disdainful comments from both readers and writers when I solicited feedback. Bad examples of the info dump abound, but are found most frequently and offensively in sequels.

I shall not embarrass their authors by naming them here, except for one author who is beyond shame because he's dead. In the Foundation series, Isaac Asimov uses articles from the *Encyclopedia Galactica* to provide readers with backstory and information he wanted the reader to know but couldn't easily or artfully weave into narrative, action, dialog tag or dialog. And, though I'm embarrassed to admit it, I've written awful, unnecessary info dumps. Now I know better.

Narratives, by the way, comprise the very dullest info dumps especially when disguised as introspection. If you write one at or near the beginning of a book chances are you won't sell it unless your track record justifies the sale.

The most annoying and insulting info dumps occur in romance series or miniseries and will often include a saccharine scene in which the heroines of the previous books get together for a lunch or coffee. The girl chat will include showing off their adorable babies and recounting the plots of past series books. This recounting is the info dump, and it is insulting in the extreme due to its lack of disguise as well as its twee, precious nature. "Remember when Trey fought the bear? Oh, I was so scared that I went straight into his arms! And that was the night that Adora, here, was conceived." Heroine bounces baby. Baby coos. Reader barfs. Book hits wall.

Not only are these passages icky but they're unnecessary. We don't need to know about Trey, the bear and Adora unless the bear appears as an antagonist in the current book.

But let me point out examples of well-written info dumps.

The entire first chapter of J. K. Rowling's *Harry Potter and the Half Blood Prince* is an info dump. Written from the point of view of the British prime minister, the chapter does an admirable job of providing the reader with the information s/he would need to understand and enjoy the sixth book of her seven book series. The writing is witty and the technique well-executed.

Forgive me for saying so, but odds are that you're not the next Rowling. You could be, and self-confidence is good in any business, especially this one. But chances are that you're not.

It's also unlikely that you're the next Charlaine Harris. In *Definitely Dead*, she gives us plenty of information to ground us in the world of Sookie Stackhouse, her companions and her loves. But Harris takes her time providing us with the information we need to understand Sookie and her life, using two chapters to weave in the data we need. There's plenty of dialog and action to keep the reader interested in the sixth book in the series.

Cassandra Clare puts a massive info dump deep into *City of Glass*, Book Three of The Mortal Instruments series. But, because we have become so immersed in her world and her characters, the info dump, disguised as a significant character's reminiscences, is not only welcome but riveting. It's an admirable example of the maxim, "make them laugh, make them cry, make them wait," variously attributed to Nora Roberts or Charles Dickens.

The information is important to the reader, revealing numerous secrets we really want to know about characters we've come to love. Emotion infuses the memories, and in a great book, emotion is always key.

Corollary of this rule:
When you provide backstory, weave it in with care

I was advised by Judy Myers, one of my first critique partners, to slip in backstory using "snippets, not chunks." She mentioned this to me in 1997. I remember that advice every time I sit down to write.

[92]

Another piece of advice: Wait. Clare's info dump fascinates rather than bores because its revelations are provided after the reader has become deeply invested in the story and the characters.

Reportedly, there are entire books published that are nothing but info dumps. Sharleen Scott wrote: "I'm also not thrilled with series authors (single title, best sellers) who use an entire book to set up future books in the series... (One) author left at least seven threads hanging. There really wasn't an ending... Books, even in a series, must have a satisfying conclusion of some sort."

There's a great piece of writerly advice out there: *Kill your darlings.*

No one's quite sure where this phrase originated, but it's been repeated often, by such notable authors as William Faulkner and Stephen King.

But it doesn't matter who originated the phrase--it's good advice. We often fall in love with our prose and are loath to cut it, especially when we may have slaved over a particularly well-turned clause or exhaustively researched, say, the eating habits of the lesser lemur of Madagascar.

But it's rare that such obscurities belong on our story, and, similarly, while we may think that providing backstory is essential, it often isn't.

Remember, info dumps are usually dull, and beside the

[93]

point, at least in a romance. Romances are about two people falling in love. Stray from that notion and you're writing something else. You may turn out a wonderful book, but it won't be a romance. When writing romance, try to keep your lovers on every page as much as possible, interacting with each other, dealing with their conflicts and creating a lasting, loving relationship.

However, writing in another genre is not a cue to indulge in info dumping. The message? Keep your eye on the ball, that is, keep in mind your characters' conflicts and goals. Don't include anything irrelevant and ***don't be boring.***

RESPECT THE ENGLISH LANGUAGE

English is a rich, varied and elegant language. From only twenty-six letters and forty-seven sounds, millions of words and concepts have been fashioned. Other languages are complicated and unwieldy by comparison. For example, Mandarin consists of thousands of characters and fifteen hundred sounds, which are modified by four tones. English is amazing. Respect it.

Corollary: Don't commit obvious errors

As writers, our language is a more important tool than our computers. Take the time to understand it. Learn grammar. Spell correctly. If you're not sure about a grammatical point or the spelling of a word, find out.

Exceptions? Of course. Dialog and introspection can convey personality traits and social status. A character who uses bad grammar may be poorly educated. When someone in one of your books often uses a cliché or a particular turn of phrase, that's a character note. And that's good. Deft use of the language shows the differences between the characters you're creating.

Small errors irritate many. Some frequently seen examples: mixing up *peeked*, *piqued* and *peaked,* as in *piqued his interest.* (A number of people noted that one). Using *that* instead of *who* or *whom*, as in "the guy that I dated in high school." A *misnomer* is not exactly the same

[95]

as a *mistake* or a *misconception* regardless of the number (not amount) of reporters who use them interchangeably.

Learn rules about apostrophe placement. If I had a nickel for each time I saw *your* when the correct word was *you're*, I'd own that villa in southern Italy I want. Comma placement is even more tricky.

I've mentioned only a few common blunders. There are probably as many ways to abuse the language as there are words in it. Learn your craft. Please.

Corollary: Avoid annoying repetitions

Authors often fall in love with words that sound special to us or are so useful we can't stop using them. Unless we have an astute editor, these repetitions are published and embarrass us forever. But don't feel bad. We've all done it.

This tendency occurs often in dialog, when we start sentences with the word "well." Yes, it's true that many people speak this way. But as noted above, we don't write dialog exactly the way people speak.

Other annoying repetitions: *feel* or its variations, *feeling* or *felt,* as in "He made her feel as though..." *Make* and *made*—also culprits, seen in the previous sentence. Okay, these are common words and we must use them, but no word or phrase should stand out because of its use or overuse.

But, as I said, we've all done it. In one of my books, I used the verbs *draw* and *drew* so frequently ("he drew his hand

[96]

up her thigh") that I'm ashamed to this day. Said Diane Farr, "In one of my books, the heroine's eyes kept 'widening.' ::wince::"

Likewise, don't overuse names. You need not tell the reader a character's name every time s/he opens his or her mouth or does something. In scenes involving two or fewer people, "he" or "she" work fine. It's the mark of a newbie to overuse names, especially in dialog.

The major exception? Scenes in which both characters are the same gender. They require the writer to employ deft phraseology to avoid continually using characters' names. Be very careful while writing these scenes, and edit with equal or greater care.

And don't repeat the same information. People read with their minds switched on. They're paying attention. Trust them. Author Autumn Jordon wrote to me that she's had to patch walls because of books she's thrown in disgust because authors tell her the same thing over and over again. "Readers are not dense," Autumn said.

Corollary: Avoid garbage words and phrases

What's wrong with this sentence?

It was Mr. Grabass who broke the silence.

I'll give you a clue: it can be rewritten with about half the words.

Still stumped? How about writing the same action like

[97]

this:

Grabass spoke first.

Eight words were cut to three, and the sentence is stronger. Why?

In the first sentence, "it" is the subject and "was" is the verb. In the second sentence, "Grabass" is the subject and "spoke" is the verb. The second sentence is more direct and clear; thus, it's stronger.

"It" isn't a character in your novel (unless you're Stephen King and wrote *It*). And "was" is simply dull. Of course, these are indispensable words, and "it was" is an indispensable phrase. But learn when they should be used and when they should be avoided. Again: neither words nor phrases should draw attention to themselves, either from use or overuse.

If you can write a shorter, snappier sentence, do so, unless you mean to write a slower scene. Long, wordy sentences will drag down the pacing and flow of your manuscript, especially when you use garbage words that don't convey anything. Remember, in this culture, fast is good and slow is bad, at least for our readers. They expect books and movies to move along. One of my respondents, Candice M. Hughes, wrote: "Fast, pulse-pounding plot is very important for me." Even the most interesting story will be dragged into the slow lane by poor word choice and bad sentence structure.

Beware of the phrases "it was" and "there was." They

usually signal careless, weak writing. "It" usually refers to another noun or object. Too many usages of that word in a paragraph generally results in a mess, because *it* will refer to more than one noun or object. That can get confusing in a hurry.

Examine the following paragraphs, which are not too different from writing I once encountered:

I freaked out when I saw how much he'd changed. It was crazy, really, but it was the most amazing transformation. It hadn't been more than a few weeks, but it had wrought the most stunning change, and it felt as though my heart had been torn asunder.

But I understood what had happened. No one encountered it remaining unchanged. It was always an experience so terrifying as to be transforming.

The overuse of *it* not only confuses but drags reader attention from the story.

The phrase "began to," as in "He began to laugh," is generally unnecessary and also weighs down sentences. "He laughed" is just fine.

As you write, watch out for phrases which describe emotion such as "she felt," and "it was as though..." They're okay to use, but don't overuse them. Ten times in every love scene is too often. They're generally are found with indirect or vague descriptions of emotion, often during intimacy, where direct is most often best, clearest and strongest.

[99]

The key to writing great genre fiction is emotion. Romances are about love. Mysteries engender curiosity. Thrillers elicit fear. Our writing should be at its best when we convey our characters' feelings.

Corollary: know your tools; use your tools

The character Robin Williams played in *Dead Poets' Society* tells his students, "Avoid using the word 'very' because it's lazy. A man is not very tired. He is exhausted. Don't use very sad, use morose."

This is excellent advice. We repeat favorite words from inattention or laziness. We use garbage phrases like "it was" because we find writing is easier if we don't have to stop and rephrase our sentence in a better, clearer, more descriptive way. This is not to say that weird words should be employed when simpler ones are available. In other words, don't use "endeavor" when "try" will do. If effort is involved, "struggle" is even better.

One of my favorite expostulations when I become tongue-tied is, "I am a writer. Words are my tools."

You are a writer. Words are your most important tools. Know your tools and how to use them.

And how not to use them.

Corollary: Avoid nouns and adjectives converted to verbs. For example, nipples do not pebble. Labia do not plump.

[100]

A pebble is a small rock, and a less appealing image than "a pebbled nipple" cannot be created. Don't be tempted to commit this sin regardless of the many times you may read this transgression. This cliché seems to be unique to romance novels, for I have never encountered a pebbled nipple elsewhere. Same with other body parts "plumping" in anticipation of sex.

Our body parts may moisten, swell, harden; they may tighten or tingle. They may do any number of things, but they do not pebble or plump.

Again, I have to admit that I do convert nouns to verbs, especially when I say, "I have to Facebook that!" Used judiciously, this technique can be a character note. But no character, even in a romance novel, has ever thought, "Oh, sexy pebbled nipples!" In your novel, a word can be used only if a character is likely to use that word.

CLICHÉS

Please do not use clichés, either verbal or situational

As stated, pebbled nipples have become a cliché of the romance genre. We can call a phrase like "pebbled nipple" a verbal cliché, that is, a turn of phrase so hackneyed as to be unforgivable. And then, we have situational clichés. What are they?

How about the "cute first meet"? An example is the heroine's car breaking down so the hero can both make her acquaintance and "rescue" her, "which she, of course, resents," says Diane Farr. "That's an important part of the cliché. In real life you'd be grateful, but romance heroines always think the rescuer is arrogant."

Yes, our hero and heroine must meet in some cute, inspiring or romantic way, but try to figure out something that's not both overused and unlikely. How probable is it that the guy who changes the heroine's flat tire later turns out to be her new boss? Not bloody likely.

Simplest is often best. Scarlett and Rhett meet at a party, as do innumerable Regency heroes and heroines. Works fine. Avoid cliché in this common plot device by creating compelling characters with interesting conflicts.

This is not to say that it's uncool to be different. In my book *Fashion Victim*, the hero sues the heroine and they meet in court. In Linda Howard's *Death Angel*, the hero

[102]

and the heroine meet when the heroine's then-boyfriend must offer her to the hero, a hitman, as the reward for a job well done.

Corollary: Avoid the hackneyed plot

Donna del Oro told me: "What turns me off to many romance novels are the recycled plots and characters. You know, the female protagonist coming back to her hometown and stumbling into/forced to work with/running from but falling for...again...a former lover/bad boy who either dumped her/left to join the Green Berets/left to pursue a fortune—and now the two face a threat worse than death...blah, blah, blah."

Keiran Brae sniffs at "the baby she had that he doesn't know is his...really?" The secret baby should go the way of the dodo. Please.

Another reader gave up on a book by "the third chapter when 1) a woman hears screams (new super hearing unexplained) at her wedding and runs to save screamer and 2) ends up in a secret BDSM underground club ACROSS the street from the local police station and 3) ends up in bed with the Dom on her supposed wedding night without thinking twice about the man she fell in love with and was supposed to MARRY!"

As for me, I avoid the plethora of serial killer books, especially when there's an FBI agent and a hot female profiler/pathetic victim involved. I recently read that authorities estimate that fewer than a hundred serial killers are at large in the United States. In other words, far more of these murderers exist in fiction than in reality. I'm tired of reading about their false activities in fear-mongering books.

CHARACTERIZATION ERRORS, OR:
People should behave like people

Corollary: Smart characters shouldn't do stupid things. No TSTL characters!

A TSTL character is a character that's Too Stupid To Live, and drew a high level of scorn from my respondents. In more than one book, characters find themselves marrying by mistake, having babies by mistake, doing all manner of things by mistake.

Granted, some of us find ourselves in the position of having to write marriages by mistake. I wrote one in a miniseries for Harlequin/Silhouette. *Engaged to the Sheik* is available digitally, and should be; that story took a lot of fancy footwork to make the plot twist successful.

But stupid stuff that's written well enough for an astute reader to accept doesn't come by very often. And how frequently have we read about smart characters doing stupid things just to advance the plot? Don't do it. It's a cheat. If you need to advance the plot, think a little harder and figure out a rational way for your characters to proceed, or at least a believable one in the context of the story you're telling.

Characters must be smart and behave intelligently, or at least consistently. While reading one book, Candice M. Hughes "felt the characters were increasingly acting in

[105]

ways contrary to their previously described personalities. The final straw came when I could 'see the strings.' I thought 'ahhh, this character has done this stupid thing because the author wants him severely injured and in the hospital. He has to be in the hospital because the author is trying to tear down his sister's previously comfortable life.' When that starts happening I feel angry and betrayed as a reader. I no longer care about the characters because they're just puppets for the author not 'people.'"

Shakespeare's *A Midsummer Night's Dream* is a good example of character craziness which is nevertheless believable. Half of his characters aren't human and most of them are subject to spells, charms or enchantments. But the irrational rationality works, even Titania's desire for the donkey-headed Bottom. Why? Because Shakespeare rooted the events in emotions we still recognize, and which his characters exhibited consistently—Oberon's stubbornness, Titania's lust, Puck's mischievousness, Helena's jealousy.

But tread carefully. There was only one Shakespeare. There won't be another.

Corollary: Misunderstandings are not conflicts; characters should behave like adults

The "non-conflict" plot also drew considerable ire. "If a simple conversation would solve everything, then there wasn't enough conflict for me in the first place," said Victoria Houseman. Kathy Crouch wrote, "I get tired of the hero and heroine so obviously misreading each other over and over and over until you are like *oh give me a break somebody talk to somebody*." L.R. Hunter agrees: "...this

[106]

would work if they were fourteen years old, but these are grown-ups!"

Corollary: Don't confuse Alpha and A-hole

We all love a strong hero. Who can forget Rhett masterfully carrying Scarlett up their mansion's grand staircase? But in so many books, we read heroes who are not heroic but abusive, men who a normal, self-respecting woman wouldn't tolerate for even a few seconds. Yet, these impossible creatures infect book after book when they belong in jail, at least in this era and culture. Victoria Houseman noted a book in which the hero was "despicable" and even the reason that he'd lost his first wife and child didn't excuse his "emotional cruelty" to the heroine and their new baby, which lasted for over 100 pages.

Want to read great alpha males? Try Linda Howard or Lisa Marie Rice. Natalie Dae and Portia Da Costa write great Dom/sub stories in which the Dom dances on the line between acceptable and awful with great dexterity.

Corollary: Don't confuse Heroine and Ho

A number of comments I read involved foul-mouthed female characters who meet the hero and promptly engage in sex without pause for thought, reflection or romance, as though the urge to procreate was "the instant itch that has to be scratched," said Daneal Cantor. Historicals author Diane Farr finds sexually careless conduct in the past was "even stupider in an era without effective birth control."

[107]

L.R. Hunter noted the following hackneyed plot: "I have read One Book by several famous authors and found that One Book to be so horrendous that I never read those authors again. 'Oh, hi, let's have sex—what was your *%^!-ing name again? No matter, when you *$^!me, I just know we're going to have our *%^!-ing HEA, because the sex was so good. Let's go shopping now, because I only have 500 *%^!-ing pairs of shoes…We can have sex in the car, in the fitting room, in the ladies' room, under the table at the food court. It'll be *%^!-ing great!'"

SETTING
Avoid the "Talking Head in the Empty Room"

I won't disguise my love of setting in the novel, nor will I apologize for it, not when entire industries have been spawned based on setting. We love the Potter books not only because we adore and admire our bespectacled hero and his sidekicks, but because we all secretly dream of shopping for our wands at Ollivander's, boarding the famous red-and-gold train, and studying at Hogwarts.

Rowling created a complete world, in ours but not quite of it, and a desire to enter that special world compels readers to reread her books many times, to watch the movies obsessively, to collect Potter memorabilia such as wands and time-turners, to visit the related theme park.

She's not alone. *Star Trek* was and is so successful that it's labeled a franchise. Though it started as a TV series, it spawned scores of books, to say nothing of additional TV series, films, conventions, computer games and even the odd telephone or fake phaser. Same with *Star Wars.*

Orson Scott Card calls fiction dependent upon setting "milieu fiction," and the best of these works include a setting so strong that it's virtually a character. For example, the architecture of Hogwarts Castle changes,

[109]

sometimes randomly, like the staircases, and sometimes according to other characters' needs, such as the Room of Requirement.

In Daphne du Maurier's *Rebecca,* Manderley is a character but not necessarily a benign one, reflecting not the narrator's personality but that of Rebecca, who, being dead, could not otherwise appear. Middle Earth, like the Wizarding World, is as important a setting in *The Hobbit* and *The Lord of the Rings* as Hogwarts Castle.

The importance of worldbuilding is not limited to paranormal fiction. The enduring popularity of Regency romance depends upon readers' love of a specific time and place, early nineteenth-century London. The Burg neighborhood of Trenton is as important as any other character in Janet Evanovich's Stephanie Plum novels. Same with Deborah Smith's Georgia or Derry, Maine, the fictitious setting of many Stephen King books.

The "Talking Head in the Empty Room" syndrome occurs when authors ignore the task of worldbuilding, which must take place while crafting every book, whether it be a thousand-word self-published short story or a weighty, multivolume epic. When I worked as an acquiring editor, I read many a story in which nothing about any setting appears until halfway through the manuscript. Guess what? I didn't buy those, not without heavy revision.

Some writers seem to assume that readers can magically perceive what's inside the author's head. We can't, and most books don't come with a crystal ball, a tarot deck or illustrations. The caveat here is stated by Rose Anderson: "You don't have to use every word in your head. When I write I see the whole picture, and I do mean **whole**. There's no need to describe everything. Four years later and my books say more with less."

The message? Ground the reader in the story with at least a few words here and there about setting, and while you're at it, use all five senses. Setting is not only what we see but what we feel, taste, smell, hear. We can scent the aroma of burned coffee and stale cigarette smoke in a well-crafted police procedural, feel the humidity and heat in Maycomb, Alabama, where Harper Lee's *To Kill a Mockingbird* is set. We hear the chilling tune of the enchanted carousel in *Something Wicked This Way Comes* (Ray Bradbury) and we're *scared*.

Setting, Ambience, and Emotion

Emotion is at the core of your story—that is, in most subgenres of popular fiction. The ambience of the setting you create can heighten, dampen, or alter reactions in whatever way contributes to the reader's experience. In *The Two Towers*, when Frodo and Sam enter Ithilien, they are greeted by:

...a fair country of climbing woods and swift-falling streams. The night became fine under star and round moon, and it seemed to the hobbits that the fragrance of the air grew as they went forward...

...All about them were small woods of resinous trees, fir and cedar and cypress, and other kinds unknown in the Shire, with wide glades among them; and everywhere there was a wealth of sweet-smelling herbs and shrubs. ... Here Spring

[111]

was already busy about them; fronds pierced moss and mould, larches were green-fingered, small flowers were opening in the turf, birds were singing. Ithilien, the garden of Gondor now desolate, kept still a disheveled dryad loveliness.

Tolkien continues in this vein for several pages. The hobbits' sojourn in Ithilien, sandwiched between their devastating failure to enter Mordor through the Black Gate and their potentially deadly encounter with Faramir and his men, is a welcome break from the tension and suspense of the quest to destroy the One Ring. Ithilien is a peaceful valley between rough crags, the eye of the storm, allowing the reader respite between threats. The ambience is light, joyous and hopeful. Along with the hobbits, the reader takes a deep breath and relaxes.

Don't squander any opportunity to heighten emotion in your novel. That includes using a setting's description to change reader reactions, as in the previous selection. And you may use the setting to mirror emotion. In *Walk Like A Man* (2006) I wrote a conversation during which the heroine tells the hero about the trauma of her mother's death, and set the scene as follows:

She was mute as he guided her toward their favorite stand of birches, which had been rendered nearly leafless by autumn winds. Their stark branches thrust toward the gray sky.

I set this book in the autumn. Had the same conversation taken place in spring, I could have used the beauty of new life as a poignant contrast to the heroine's grief and guilt. My point? Setting can almost always be used to heighten

[112]

emotion. Don't pass by this valuable opportunity to deepen your readers' experience of your story.

OTHER MATTERS

The Dull Denouement

In a debut book by an otherwise wonderful author, the hero and the heroine solved their conflicts and defeated the bad guy about two-thirds of the way through the book. Unfortunately, one-third of the book was left. All manner of unnecessary events were shoveled in, possibly to bring the word count to the length of a standard single title. We met the parents. We endured an engagement party...mercifully, the fog of memory has obscured the remainder of the horrifying banality. I prayed for the villain to rise from the dead and attack, but no such luck.

The major conflicts should be resolved in one climactic scene. Then your hero and heroine should quickly sail into the sunset to live happily ever after.

Even great writers can commit this misstep. In J.R.R. Tolkien's classic *Lord of the Rings* (*Return of the King*), the One Ring is destroyed and Sauron defeated on page 957 (of the Houghton-Mifflin hardcover edition published in 2002). The End, right? Wrong. In the movie, there's a pretty good denouement. Not perfect, but pretty good. In the book, nearly 100 pages remain, far too many even with the scouring of the Shire. (I am not counting the Appendices).

But the opposite is equally bad. In Patricia Cornwell's *In Potter's Field*, Kay Scarpetta dispatches the villain, a vicious serial killer, on page 411 of the hardcover. The book ends three paragraphs later. When I first read it, I found myself staring at that last page, trying by force of will to make the denouement longer. I felt incomplete. I didn't experience that "ahhhh…" we all want when the characters have defeated the forces of evil and won their battles, whether with themselves, each other or a villain.

"I hate investing 350 pages into a book with a good premise, characters I like, (and) a suspenseful plot only to have the ending rushed," said Maureen Rumsey. Barbara Phinney believes that "writers need to ensure the ending is top notch and doesn't slack off." She was one of the few who believes that a happily ever after ending isn't essential, stating, "I also like endings that aren't everyone getting along happily. That's not realistic."

For most of this era's romance readers, a happily ever after (HEA) ending is obligatory, but historically, that's not the case. In the early romances, tragedy was the norm, with a hopeless love at center stage. Examples are *Romeo and Juliet,* or the tale of Tristan and Iseult. Perhaps these stories, as well as those from the modern era, reflect readers' expectations about their own lives. In the early days of romance, people wed for economic rather than emotional reasons. Love and desire were found outside marriage.

Comments indicate that some readers may be ready for an expansion of the genre, though I don't know what, if any, societal change has prompted this shift. It just may be that avid readers are bored by HEA.

[115]

In *Novelist's Essential Guide to Crafting Scenes,* Raymond Obstfeld writes that the ending to a novel is "like a debriefing." Good examples of well-written denouements abound. They're not difficult, which makes errors one way or the other tough to excuse. Look at almost every Sherlock Holmes mystery—or most mysteries, for that matter. There's usually a scene after the main action is over in which we find ourselves in the comfortable, familiar environs of 221B Baker Street, with Holmes in his robe and slippers, puffing on a pipe and explaining all to Watson. No more is necessary, but such a scene is indispensable.

Draft and Edit

Most of us take great pride in our work, and we won't send out anything to a critique partner that hasn't been polished to the nth degree, self-edited and re-edited. By the time a manuscript gets to an agent or publisher, the work should be damn near perfect.

Make sure that there are no continuity glitches, such as one that Laurie Anderson identified for me, when a character picked up her iPhone, indulged in three paragraphs of introspection, and picked up her iPhone again. She didn't drop her phone, nor did she own two.

Avoid the non-chronological sentence or paragraph structure, noted by L.R. Hunter, which is like an unsettling mini-flashback: "Before eating her muffin, she sorted the mail and balanced her checkbook."

Do your research. Maureen Rumsey identified a book in which the hero—supposedly a wilderness guide—warns the heroine of poisonous snakes in an area where there are none; worse, the hero and the heroine wander for days in an area of western Washington that isn't wilderness but subdivisions. "Impossible for anyone but a complete moron."

Don't write stupid stuff, such as a heroine taking a long horseback ride around her six-acre ranch, noted by Barbara Phinney. (I suppose that the heroine could own that dubious property called a "ranchette," but it's more likely that both the writer and the editor blew it). Or when a murder victim suddenly begins speaking—and the book isn't a paranormal. Barbara needed several rereadings to realize that the names of the victim and the hero had been transposed.

This kind of error occasionally does slip through the editorial process, but nevertheless is very difficult for readers to forgive. You'll lose fans.

Items I Haven't Discussed

Adverbs: Adverbs modify verbs in the same way that adjectives modify nouns, adding a little extra meaning. Overuse of adjectives is frowned upon, but any use at all of adverbs is considered a mortal sin by many. In fact, I heard one editor state at a conference that she didn't want to see a single word in a manuscript that ended in *ly* unless the heroine's name was Emily.

My opinion? They're okay. Don't overuse them. If I had a

dime for the number of times Rowling wrote, as a dialog tag, "Hermione said keenly" I'd be wealthy.

Note that this craft flaw has not held Rowling back.

Exclamation points and italics: Don't overuse them. The writing should provide the emphasis you want to convey. Even once or twice in a chapter is probably too often.

Prepositional phrases: They're okay. Don't overuse them. Especially avoid a string, i.e., She raced to fetch the treasure that had been buried in the corner under the bricks in the old brass box during the snowstorm of 1898.

William Zinnser and others think that prepositional phrases shouldn't be used at the beginning of a sentence as they weaken the main action. Pish-tosh, I say. Use them occasionally to vary sentence structure.

This is a matter of taste. As I've stated, there are styles and fashions in writing just as in many other undertakings. A good example relates to point of view: when Austen and Dickens wrote, long narratives in the third person omniscient point of view (POV) were common and accepted. These days, we don't care for them.

Same with the use of adverbs and prepositional phrases.

What makes a good book?

Opinions weren't completely uniform on this question. "A great book is one that captures my attention in the first chapter," says Robin Hillyer Miles. She prefers "a book with flawed characters who learn something about themselves by the book's end, set in a location that is recognizable."

"A heroine who's not a Mary Sue, but who isn't Courtney Love, either," says L.R. Hunter. "A hero who has the bone-deep goodness to be a lifetime husband. Conflict that keeps them apart, that isn't caused by silly misunderstandings, but that can be overcome or managed or turned into a positive. Snappy (not snippy) dialog, honest emotions, economic and social conditions that ring true. A writing voice that is fun, but not overwhelming. Clarity."

Candice M. Hughes prefers a different kind of book. "Everything has to click: a fast, big plot that is believable (with) interesting, believable, consistent characters."

Alert readers of this article have already noticed that *emotion* has popped up here and there. Remember the reason *A Midsummer Night's Dream* works? The craziness is rooted in the characters' emotions. And I mentioned that romances are about emotions. *All great stories are memorable because they elicit emotional responses from readers.* We want the good guys to defeat the baddies, Dorothy to get back to Kansas and, despite her flaws, we want Scarlett to succeed. When Juliet dies, we suffer Romeo's pain and loss. If a man loves a woman, it's a reason to rejoice.

But creating that response is easier said than done. Good craft helps.

[119]

We all want to read quality books, not manuscripts that don't exhibit the craftsmanship we have come to expect.

Write. Be critical of yourself. Use critique partners and contests to hone your work. Don't be afraid to cut, squeeze and trim; your words aren't Holy Writ. Then write and edit some more.

And you and your characters will live happily ever after.

APPENDIX ONE:

On Synopsis

Often referred to as "the dreaded synopsis" by many writers, the importance of this document has been greatly overstated. When I've worked as an acquiring editor, I didn't want "my" writers to waste too much time on these, because the synopsis will never be published. I'd rather authors worked harder on their manuscripts.

Still, a synopsis is a chance to strut your stuff, and those few pages (no more than two to four in my opinion, unless the book is a multivolume epic) it should be thoroughly self-edited and polished.

It should contain a brief blurb summarizing the main idea, story or theme of the book, with a sentence about setting. It should then describe the main characters and their conflicts, and provide a brief précis of the story.

And that's all. I didn't care how the author provided this information as long as it's spellchecked and grammatical. For example, the below would be acceptable:

Title: The Great American Novel
Setting: Manhattan, 2154
Genre: futuristic romance

Heroine: Francesca Futuregrrl, an orphaned cyborg searching for love but hampered by inner conflicts surrounding her dubious past as a Petri dish baby and her inability to bear children.

Hero: Gus Grizzled, a tough-but tender cop reeling from his role in his partner's "accidental" death, which took place when Gus's ray-gun exploded.

Blurb: blah-blah-blah, but ideally fewer than 25 words

Plot précis: more blah-blah.

Get the picture? Don't agonize over it. Save the angst for the book.

APPENDIX TWO:
Advice from Other Authors

I asked a few of my online friends to tell me what advice they would have given their younger selves about the craft of writing. Here are a few snippets:

There are so many things I wish I'd known, but the one I'll say is Scene and Sequel.
Joan Reeves

It will take you eight novels to learn how to write well and be ready to publish, so begin now!
Rolynn Anderson

It's never too late to start writing. Remember artist Grandma Moses who didn't begin her career until she was 78 then produced over 2,000 paintings.

Diane Burton

It's hard work but you'll make it if you keep at it.
Calisa Rhose

Finish your first draft! You will learn more about your process, your strengths, and your weaknesses by doing this than you will ever learn in classes and workshops.
Rachel Smith

There is such a steep learning curve to conquer--no, *multiple* steep learning curves to conquer--that you really can't get into this game unless you have real passion for writing. The financial rewards are slim relative to the effort that goes into producing a book.
Maggie Le Page

Don't listen to one negative person. Seek more opinions. You know what you have written is good, and others will see it, too. Just don't stop writing! In the following years, you will even improve. You know what they say about practice!
Jan Carol

Take a screenwriting course to learn about story structure to help with plotting. I took a 6 week college course that was a huge help.
Kathy Kulig

APPENDIX THREE:
From Chapter One, *Lord Devere's Ward*

Badham Abbey, Wiltshire, England
January, 1820

"God, help me!"

Kate Scoville kicked and flailed her feet, struggling to grip the tower wall with her oversized boots. She whispered a hasty prayer in the chance that the Almighty paid attention to her small corner of His world. Wearing clumsy, borrowed gloves, she grasped the rope tied to the attic window and pushed her boots against the side of the tower, seeking purchase on the wall.

At last, her toes found a mortared joint between two massive blocks of stone. She breathed deeply until her racing pulse steadied. The chill air knifed her lungs. She could see her breath, small puffy clouds, when she exhaled.

She looked down and gulped. Three far stories below her, the slate roof of the abbey gleamed, pale and frosty in the moonlight.

She tried not to utter curses damning her wretched uncle, whose treachery had brought her to such desperate straits. First he'd torn her away from her beloved home in Somerset. Then he'd nagged her to marry his beef-witted son, Osborn, until she thought he'd drive her quite out of her mind. Locking her in an icy tower attic until she cooperated had been the proverbial last straw.

She inched her boots down the tower wall. The short sword she wore on her belt beat against her side with every halting step as her cape flapped around her knees.

She finally attained her immediate goal: the abbey's second-story roof. Still clasping the rope, she crept across the slippery slates. If she reached the edge of the roof without mishap, she'd climb down to the ground by way of a convenient vine or tree.

At the end of the rope, she released it with a shaky, nervous hand. A few steps later, her feet flew out from under her. Yelping, she fell with a bump to slide down the pitched roof, scrabbling for a hold.

Scant feet from the brink, she plunged into a black gap. Her cape caught on the rough edges and timbers of the roof, breaking her fall. Despite her clinging garb, she plummeted through the hole, too shocked and frightened to scream.

"Oof!" She landed on a wooden floor, which emitted a massive boom as she hit. Her body clenched, and she whimpered in mingled fear and pain, realizing she could have been badly hurt had she fallen on her sword. She rubbed her left side through her doublet. She'd be bruised the next day, but didn't have time to sit and bemoan her aches and pains.

Heat from her exertions flooded her body. She controlled her trembling, stood, and then looked about, recognizing the ballroom on the abbey's second floor. She adjusted her borrowed clothing, the costume of a Tudor boy she'd found in the attic. She'd donned it knowing that a doublet, hose, boots, and cape were more practical garb for escaping from a locked tower room than her usual bulky gown and soft shoes.

She prayed that no one had been awakened by her noisy advent into the cavernous ballroom. The entire household should have

[125]

been roused by the din she'd made. Perhaps God did listen.

Kate smoothed her hair with a quivering hand whilst considering her situation. She was tired, sore, and frightened, but she was now only one floor away from freedom. She could leave through any of the large windows lining the ballroom to climb down to the ground. She wasn't sufficiently bold as to use the front door.

She twisted the latch of the nearest window, pushing it outward. The hinges squealed, an unnerving sound which kicked up her heartbeat to a gallop.

But still, no one was roused. No one raised an alarm. With relief, she remembered the sordid habits of her uncle and his whelp. Herbert and Osborn were undoubtedly sleeping off last night's libations. The servants, as undisciplined as their masters, were doubtless in no better condition.

How could her grandfather have made such a foolish choice? She'd lived with him since the deaths of her parents, and surely he must have been aware of Herbert's predilections. The odd arrangement her grandfather had created in his Will left her in her uncle's custody until her coming-out, but had made her the ward of an Earl in faraway London, an older fellow she'd met but once. "Grandfather must have gone dotty at the end," she muttered.

She cast aside her fruitless reflections. Stepping through the open window to the terrace outside, she flipped a leg over the balustrade near a pillar, which was covered by a sturdy ivy vine. Digging a boot between its twining, woody stems, she used it as her ladder to reach the snowy ground below.

She dashed over the snow without a backward look, hoping that no one from the house observed her dark shape stumbling across the bright, white field. The front gate was locked, but she found a spot where the current Earl had neglected the upkeep of the walls. She grinned when she saw the tumbledown stones, which proved to be an easy climb.

She headed for the tollgate near Derbeck. All coaches and stages traveling west to Bath or east to London would stop there.

But where would she go?

* * *

Kate hesitated as she regarded the imposing door fronting the Earl of Devere's Berkeley Square townhouse. She hoped that her guardian could relieve her anxiety. She'd felt little else since she'd embarked upon her current perilous course by setting her boots against the frosty stone wall of Badham Abbey's tower attic.

She drew her hood back. Her hair, untended for days, threatened to slip from its ribbon, and she pushed it out of her face. Lifting the heavy brass knocker, she let it fall. Its boom echoed the frightened pounding of her heart...

SELECTED REFERENCES

Bickham, Jack: Writing Novels that Sell (1989)
Brown, Rita Mae: *Starting from Scratch* (1989 softcover edition)
Browne and King: Self-Editing for Fiction Writers (1993)
Campbell, Joseph: Hero With a Thousand Faces (1949)
King, Stephen: *On Writing* (2000)
Obstfeld, Raymond: Novelist's Essential Guide to Crafting Scenes (2000)
Vogler, Christopher: *The Writer's Journey* (1992)

I used many sources on the internet for information, and some information and quotes came from here:

http://www.theatlantic.com/entertainment/archive/2013/07/why-stephen-king-spends-months-and-even-years-writing-opening-sentences/278043/

http://grammar.about.com

http://www.be-a-better-writer.com/scenes-and-sequels.html

http://www.jennycrusie.com/info/faqs/

http://en.wikipedia.org/wiki/Chapter_(books)

http://www.slate.com/blogs/browbeat/2013/10/18/_kill_your_darlings_writing_advice_what_writer_really_said_to_murder_your.html

ACKNOWLEDGMENTS

With thanks to the many authors who contributed their thoughts and ideas:

Diane Farr, www.dianefarrbooks.com/
Kylie Brant, http://www.kyliebrant.com
Jennifer Crusie, http://www.jennycrusie.com/
Eileen Dreyer, http://www.eileenddreyer.com
Phyllis Humphrey, http://www.phyllishumphrey.com
Silver James, http://www.silverjames.com
Cassie Ryan, http://www.cassieryan.com
Dee Brice, http://www.deebrice.com
Cheryl Norman, www.cherylnorman.com/
Judy Ashley
Nick Roberts, http://masternickroberts.wordpress.com/
Loucinda McGary, www.loucindamcgary.com
Sharleen Scott
Donna del Oro, www.donnadeloro.com
Keiran Brae, www.keiranbrae.com
Victoria Houseman, www.victoriahouseman.com
Candice Hughes, www.candicehughes.com
Kathy Crouch, ckcrouch.wordpress.com/
LR Hunter, www.lrhunter.com
Daneal Cantor
Robin Hillyer Miles, www.itsalways933.com
Autumn Jordon, www.AutumnJordon.com
Maureen Rumsey
Barbara Phinney, www.barbaraphinney.com
Laurie Anderson
Rose Anderson http://calliopeswritingtablet.com/

Joan Reeves, http://www.joanreeves.com
Rolynn Anderson, http://www.rolynnanderson.com
Kathy Kulig, http://www.kathykulig.com
Diane Burton, http://www.dianeburton.com
Calisa Rhose, www.calisarhose.com
Rachel Smith, www.rachelleighsmith.com
Maggie Le Page, http://www.maggielepage.com
Jan Carol, http://www.jancarolromancenovels.weebly.com

About the Author

Suz deMello says, "I'm a cliche... A vegan yoga teacher from California who loves walks on the beach, cuddling her dogs and writing romance novels." But she's an award-winning, best-selling writer who's hit several best-seller lists, been short-listed for the RITA, and reviewed by such prestigious publications such as *Kirkus, Library Journal,* and *Publisher's Weekly.*

Her books are fast paced, with seductive situations, complicated characters. She has written about two dozen books (frankly, she's lost count) and co-authored many more. Her genres include nonfiction, romance, erotica, comedy, historical, paranormal, mystery and suspense. She has also written numerous short stories and articles on writing.

She uses a pseudonym to protect her privacy. But if you're a romance fan, you've probably read her books or have heard of her, since she's known for layered, compelling novels charged with humor as well as emotion.

Her personal motto is: "Never stop learning, never stop growing." She has earned a 2d degree black belt in kenpo karate and has had at least six careers she can remember, including librarian, trial attorney, Starbucks barista, grant writer, and yoga teacher. Perhaps her most interesting career move was teaching English to preschoolers in China.

She's left the US over a dozen times, including lengthy stints working overseas. She's now living in Mexico, where she walks on the beach and cuddles her dogs every day.

[131]

She welcomes comments and reviews of all her books. Any suggestions that will improve *About Writing* are especially appreciated.

Find her books at www.suzdemello.com

For editing services, email her at suzdemello@gmail.com

Befriend her on Facebook: www.facebook.com/SuzDeMello

She tweets @suzdemello

Goodreads: bit.ly/SuzATGoodreads

Her current blog is The Velvet Lair.com